"*Deep faith is not only for the religious professic*
institutional religion - it's for the 'clients' of the (
pews. Attorney and committed Christian Lyn Robbins writes about the life of vibrant,
traditional Christianity in this book. If your faith is centered in a rich, robust experience
of traditional Church-centered Christianity, you will want to read In the Court of the
Master."

> --- Dr. Merrill Hawkins, Associate Professor of Counseling and Religion,
> Director - Spiritual Guidance and Care Program, Carson-Newman College

"*Lyn Robbins draws on his life experience as a Christ follower, lay teacher, lawyer, and*
loyal friend to encourage and challenge both seekers and believers. His reflections affirm
honest questions about faith and celebrate life lived in pure, simple devotion to Christ."

> --- Dr. Jason B. Rogers,
> Vice President for Administration and University Counsel, Belmont University

"*To read* In the Court of the Master *is to sit down next to Lyn Robbins in a pew after*
church. (He would have been in the choir during the worship service.) Sit with him here,
as you read, and have a conversation about what you've just experienced in worship and
how it might make a difference tomorrow at work. Lyn is a musician; clues are present
throughout the book. Lyn is a lay theologian; testimony to that fact can be found on
almost every page. Lyn is a professional attorney; there's evidence from cover to cover.
You and the questions that follow you home from church have found a friend in Lyn
Robbins."

> --- Dr. Terry W. York, Professor of Christian Ministry and Church Music,
> George W. Truett Seminary

"*Lyn has given us in this book fodder for our thoughts about how we can struggle*
meaningfully with our own inadequacies and doubts that arise in our walk in life and
in faith. He wisely articulates why it's okay not to always have neatly boxed and gift
wrapped answers to all the spiritual questions with which we may wrestle. This is a
book for those who embrace faith and seek to grow - and who are not satisfied with the
shallows of faith."

> --- Bradley J.B. Toben, Dean, Baylor University School of Law

IN THE COURT OF THE MASTER

An Ordinary Man's Walk With An Extraordinary God

Lyn Robbins

In the Court of the Master
An Ordinary Man's Walk With An Extraordinary God

Published by Austin Brothers Publishing

Keller, Texas

www.austinbrotherspublishing.com

ISBN 978-0-9819023-5-7

Austin Brothers
Publishing

Printed in the United States of America

2011 -- First Edition

In the Court of the Master *is dedicated to the memory of my grandfathers, C.F. Wellborn and J.L. Robbins. Granddaddy modeled what it is to be a Christian lawyer. Papa often did not accept the common explanations offered for what he saw in the world around him. Their influence is all over this book, although I did not realize it very much or appreciate it properly as I was writing.*

Acknowledgments

I am grateful to many who helped in getting these thoughts to the page. Bryan Richardson, who gave me some of my earliest preaching opportunities, has been a constant source of encouragement and took on the job of reading the manuscript and making it better. Opportunities for me to begin to collect thoughts like these, write them down, and deliver them to various audiences have been provided over the years by Debra Jackson, Mark Edwards, Dan Francis, Jeff Simmons, Frank Lewis, David Benjamin, John Parker, Michael Cox, Fran Patterson, Terry York, Tom Fettke, and others who apparently have seen something in me. The spiritual formation influence that Jim Gallery and Joe Morrell have had on my life cannot be overstated. Encouragement when I was ready to junk the whole idea of writing a book has come, at just the right times, from my wife Gena, Randy Smith, Charlie Johnson, and my daughter Annessa. My editor Terry Austin has thoughtfully put a bow on all of this. Thanks to you all.

Several of my friends are mentioned and cited somewhere in these pages – some with permission, some not. Some of you will be very surprised to find your names here. I hope I quoted you correctly (I tried!), and I hope you like what I have done with your words and ideas.

How anybody functions without a loving and supportive family is beyond me. My wife and kids have patiently listened to unedited bits and pieces of these chapters over the years, and they have let me sit at the computer and type when perhaps I had more pressing family duties that I should have been fulfilling. My parents, Dr. Wayne and Dr. Faye Robbins – who are both seminarians, writers, and university professors – read every word and offered their sage advice and experience. Gena, Trey, Carolyn, Annessa, Mom, and Dad – I love and treasure you all more than I say.

Contents

Foreword

As will be obvious to you when you begin reading this book, I am not a preacher. I have not been to seminary, I do not read Greek or Hebrew, and I am not sure what the word *homiletics* means.

I am just an ordinary guy, a working stiff. I happen to be a lawyer, conditioned by training and experience to look for answers, resolutions, and rules. What is more important is that I am a believer, a man who is a part of the real world trying as best I can to work through this thing called "faith" as I seek to become a better disciple. I confess to being frustrated when I cannot find a ready answer to every question or a rule to follow for each turn in life's road.

To those of us unwilling to accept the pat answers we sometimes get in Sunday School, there is a seemingly infinite number of questions surrounding our religion. I am convinced that there are answers to most of those questions for those who have the wisdom and the patience and the imagination to hear God's responses to our wonderings. I do not pretend that these pages hold answers for everyone.

My language is the language of scripture and hymns, translated through the culture of our day. Scripture and hymns have defined much of my life, and the culture is where destiny has brought me now. Perhaps you speak some of the same languages. If so, you will at least be at home with my word choices, and you will understand some references that others will miss.

I think that God is in this work. I know He has been in the writing and the organizing of it, for I feel His hand on mine. I pray that He will join you in your reading as well.

THOUGHTS ON DISCIPLESHIP

The Master-Servant Relationship and God's Donkeys

One of the most important and pervasive concepts in the law is that of the master-servant relationship. Many states have updated the terminology to "employment law" or some other phrase, but the meaning is the same. There are masters, and there are servants. As Bob Dylan sang, you've got to serve somebody.

Following Christ calls for service and for our constant recognition of Him as master. That is why we use the word Lord. It is what "discipleship" is all about.

Serve is one of the words that lifelong Christians have used since we were small children first learning about Jesus. We sang, "Serve Him, serve Him all ye little children," and we heard about serving others. As we grew older, we began memorizing scripture, and sooner or later we got to Romans 12:1 and had the phrase "which is your reasonable service" ingrained in our memory.

Somewhere along the way, many of us apparently grow out of the ideal of service for the Lord. That is odd because we continue to pray to be of service. How many prayers have you heard in church or blessings at the dinner table that include the words, often right after blessing the food, "bless us to thy service?"

What an interesting prayer.

Have you ever felt that God was calling you to do something but you did not have the first clue how to do it? Have you wanted desperately to serve but felt powerless to do so? Have you decided that service is for other people who have talents and abilities that you do not have?

You are absolutely right. You do not have the first clue about how to serve as the Master served. You are completely powerless to take on the mantle He has for you. You have neither the talents nor the abilities to do what God has called you to do.

What you do have is God's Holy Spirit.

Scripture is often not subtle. Another one of those early memory verses is Acts 1:8, which tells us that we shall receive power. When? We shall receive power after the Holy Spirit has come upon us. He is our power source. When we realize that we have no idea what to do or how to proceed, that we are weak and powerless, and that we have nothing within us to enable us to answer God's call to service, it is then that His magnificent power is made complete in us, and we rise to heights not contemplated before. Steven Curtis Chapman sings that "His strength is perfect when our strength is gone."

Our power comes from the Holy Spirit, who strengthens us as we admit our weakness. Every single believer is gifted by the Holy Spirit with one or more supernatural attributes given for the purpose of building up the church. Some of the gifts are listed in various places in the New Testament, and I am not going to take this space to make an exhaustive catalog of them all. They include things like wisdom, teaching, leadership, mercy, giving, prophecy, and discernment of spirits. What is important is that while you do not have all of them – the only person ever to walk the earth with all of the gifts of the Spirit was Jesus Christ – you most assuredly have one or more of them if you are a Christian. Do not take excessive pride in your gift, for it is not of your own making; but do not put on a sad face and announce that you have no gift either, for in doing so you deny what the Holy Spirit Himself has entrusted to you.

We Christians are all part of the body of Christ, the way that Christ moves and speaks and is seen and heard in the world. If you are an eye, do not be upset that you are not a foot. What would the foot be without the eye? What would the hand be without the foot? You have a great role to play, and the Spirit has gifted you and empowered you to play that role so that the church can function and Christ's work can be done.

That is what we call service. We are in the classic master-servant relationship, and He is assuredly the master. That leaves only one role – servant – for each of us.

The obvious question that is left, then, is what will God call you to do? You may not have heard a call to preach or the call to missions in the Amazon valley or even that call to teach a Sunday School class. How can you know that He is calling you to any service at all? Moses, standing at the burning bush and holding the rod that would soon become a hissing snake, asked the question this way: "What do I have in my hand that you can use, God?"

It is not for me to answer that question. That is between you and God. Remember that He calls you and He empowers you.

I once heard pastor Dan Yeary tell the story of a young boy walking along a desert cliff. The boy came upon some men looking over the cliff, apparently having lost something of immense value. When they saw the boy, they offered him a great deal of money to let them tie a rope around his waist so that they could hold him while he went over the side of the cliff to retrieve their lost item. Without a word, the boy left, only to return a few minutes later with a very old man. The boy said, "Now I will do what you want, but only if my father holds the rope."

Are you willing to let Him hold your rope?

Since "service" is what we have heard in church since we sang our first song, it is not original to remind us of our need to serve. What may be original and surprising is the understanding that the best and most faithful servants in the Bible were neither the apostles nor the angels. Instead, the ones that teach us the most about working in the service of God are scripture's donkeys.

There are actually a number of good donkey stories in the Bible. There must have been donkeys on Noah's Ark. We grew up singing about friendly beasts admiring the Christ child in the manger. It is not hard to imagine the first hee-haw in the Garden of Eden as the original donkey waited to be named. Donkeys, after all, are (along with oxen) the only animals named in the Ten Commandments – you must not covet them.

I want to touch briefly on three biblical donkey stories, because I think they go a long way to teach us how God works in our lives. The question you should be asking yourself is, "Which donkey am I?"

You may have guessed the first story, since it is about the best press that donkeys have ever received. It is the story of Balaam. You see, Balaam was a prophet who was tuned in to God's frequency, and God would periodically use Balaam as a conduit to speak to His people. As Moses approached the land of Moab, the king of that land offered Balaam a substantial sum to come and curse the Israelites. In spite of God's warnings, Balaam headed off to do the deed.

He had not gone far when his donkey left the road, crossed a field, fell down, and refused to get up. Balaam beat the poor beast with his cane three times; then suddenly, the donkey began to speak! She told Balaam that he should be ashamed of himself for beating her, since all she had done was to try to save his life! Then an angel appeared with a flaming sword and told Balaam that he would indeed have been dead if the donkey had not veered off the road to avoid where the angel stood, sent by God to stop Balaam's mission. Needless to say, Balaam promised to follow God's suggestions from then on!

Lost somewhere in the outcome of Balaam's repentance and Moses' march is the wonder I feel when I realize that God, in a remarkable display of His power and His control, chose to use a talking donkey.

The second donkey story is part of the history of one of our most significant Christian holidays. It is from the New Testament, although it springs from an Old Testament prophecy.

And when they had approached Jerusalem and had come to Bethphage, to the Mount of Olives, then Jesus sent two disciples, saying to them, "Go into the village opposite you, and immediately you will find a donkey tied there and a colt with her; untie them, and bring them to Me. "And if anyone says something to you, you shall say, 'The Lord has need of them,' and immediately he will send them." Now this took place that what was spoken through the prophet might be fulfilled, saying, "Say to the daughter of Zion, 'Behold your King is coming to you, gentle, and mounted on a donkey, even on a colt, the foal of a beast of burden.'" And the disciples went and did just as Jesus had directed them, and brought the donkey and the colt, and laid on them their garments, on which He sat. And most of the multitude spread their garments in the road, and others were cutting branches from the trees, and spreading them in the road. And the multitudes going before Him, and those who followed after were crying out, saying, "Hosanna to the Son of David. Blessed is He who comes in the name of the Lord. Hosanna in the highest!" (Matthew 21:1-9, NAS)

This was a special donkey, one prophesied by Zechariah, who was to carry the Master on His final triumphant ride into Jerusalem. Jesus was a man who walked virtually everywhere He went. On that special, triumphant Sunday, though, He would ride. On that Sunday, there was a particular donkey colt that was waiting for Him, tied with its mother, waiting to be the proud bearer of the savior of the world.

I doubt the young donkey knew that it was going to be a special day, and I doubt that he had the slightest idea who Zechariah was, but somehow I think he knew that his rider that day was someone very special.

The last story is quite familiar, although we do not generally think of the donkey as the obvious object lesson from it.

And it came to pass in those days, that there went out a decree from Caesar Augustus, that all the world should be taxed. (And this taxing was first made when Cyrenius was governor of Syria.) And all went to be taxed, every one into his own city. And Joseph also went up from Galilee, out of the city of Nazareth, into Judaea, unto the city of David, which is called Bethlehem; (because he was of the house and lineage of David) to be taxed with Mary his espoused wife, being great with child. And so it was, that, while they were there, the days were accomplished that she should be delivered. And she brought forth her firstborn son, and wrapped him in swaddling clothes, and laid him in a manger; because there was no room for them in the inn. (Luke 2:1-7, KJV)

Notice the donkey, which (at least according to song and story) carried the pregnant Mary from Nazareth to Bethlehem, does not warrant a single word in the gospel. I remember singing in a Christmas musical when I was in about the sixth grade, and one of the songs was called "Clip Clop Clop Clip," about the donkey bearing Mary, who was "great with child," to Bethlehem. But Luke, who is excited to tell us about shepherds and angels, does not mention the donkey.

I think that God wants to use us in just the same ways that He used the donkeys of scripture. Occasionally, for a very few, God chooses to make us an instrument of earth-shattering events and miraculous wonders. We may find ourselves doing things far beyond our capabilities or expectations. Those lucky few will assuredly get great press… right up there with the talking donkey.

For others, God has a special role reserved for us that has been laid out in His blueprint from before the beginning of time. We may not know that that day has come, and we may be clueless as to how our work for Him fits into the cosmic scheme. When the appointed moment arrives, however, we know that there is someone special along for the ride, and we understand that somehow we have been chosen to be the bearer of good news.

For most of us, though, our labor in God's service appears very ordinary. In fact, we might not get mentioned at all. We simply blend into the setting. We are just a strong back helping a needy person with a heavy burden. We may not think we matter.

Oh how we matter! What wonderful things God has in store for His people! Yes, we may not get earthly mention, but nobody is just "background" to God. He joyfully prepares each of His children for a unique role in His master plan. For every talking donkey among us there must be millions of strong backs to carry the loads of the world and become the bearers of things that we cannot imagine. The person we help, nothing more than another unmarried pregnant girl to the world, is, in the eyes of those who will take the time to see, the very mother of God.

What a privilege it is for us nameless donkeys to play any part, no matter how apparently insignificant to those writing the history books, in such a divine moment!

What donkey are you? I do not know. Maybe you do not know yet either. I do know this – you are one of them. Whether it is for an amazing miracle or a single triumphant moment or a trip down an ordinary highway, it is for His wonderful, unique, amazing, world-changing design.

Do not worry if you are not a talking donkey. That just means that you are on the road to Bethlehem.

The Tax Code Of Heaven – What Does God Require?

One of the law school classes that I have not had to use professionally was income tax. Of course, like everyone else, I have to pay income tax, so I have kept up with the concept, even if I don't often have to advise clients about taxes.

We have a tax code that requires us to pay a certain percentage of our income and our wealth to the government. There is a constitutional amendment allowing the government to take our money from us, and we cannot avoid it.

Unfortunately, too many people think of God as a glorified IRS agent, just waiting to audit us and requiring that we legalistically give a set amount in order to keep Him off our backs.

I am a tither. I believe in offerings, and I am living proof that God honors those who give from the firstfruits of the blessings God has given them. I try hard to be a cheerful giver.

But that is not what God requires. He wants it, He honors it, and He blesses it, but what He requires – what must be paid – is something quite different. In fact, material giving would be a lot easier. To the Old Testament complainers, getting away with giving livestock or precious oil would have solved a lot of spiritual dilemmas.

God asks for something else. When our spiritual "tax return" is filled out and sent in, God examines our hearts.

With what shall I come before the LORD
and bow down before the exalted God?
Shall I come before him with burnt offerings,
with calves a year old?
Will the LORD be pleased with thousands of rams,
with ten thousand rivers of oil?
Shall I offer my firstborn for my transgression,
the fruit of my body for the sin of my soul?
He has showed you, O man, what is good.
And what does the LORD require of you?
To act justly and to love mercy
and to walk humbly with your God. (Micah 6:6-8, NIV)

Milestones come to all of us in different forms. I have passed milestones in terms of birthdays, graduation ceremonies, and births. One I shall never forget is the first time I drove my son and his girlfriend to a movie. As milestones roll past, it is time to look back, to explore the future, and to evaluate what God requires of me.

As Christians, contemplation of our future ultimately centers on the hope of gathering at the river. In the meantime, though, when we evaluate our commitment to Him as we make that march toward Zion, we cannot conscientiously conclude that we are anything other than sinful creatures found wanting. I look at the forty-plus years of my life and see a lot of black marks and wasted time. I want to make up for all of it right now.

We find ourselves seeking supernatural brownie points by approaching a self-discovered "tax time" and giving things, instead of ourselves, to God. As if God could really be pleased by things… as if He needs anything. Too often, our first impulse is ritualistic, approaching God with our ultra-modern burnt offerings of tithes and church attendance, volunteer hours and gifts to charity. When we realize that is not enough, we look for our best, most valuable *things* to offer. To the ancient Israelites, a year old calf was an extravagant offering, since such a calf had not yet been used for all that its owner could get out of it before being sacrificed. If we are not being what God requires of us, we too look for another thing to offer.

Since God aims for who we are, not what we have or what we do, even very good gifts are insufficient by themselves. Like the gift of Cain, such offerings are not pleasing to God. Our response, like that of Micah's ancient audience, can pass quickly to the ridiculous: "OK, God, if that is not enough, how about a thousand rams, or maybe ten thousand rivers of oil? Maybe that will satisfy you." By the time we accuse God of requiring our firstborn, we have convinced ourselves that He is impossible to please and that we might as well quit trying. Our milestones become millstones, sinking us in wells of self-pity and frustration.

It is impossible to please God by giving Him things. What He wants *is* what we are and what we can become. Even if we give everything we have to the poor, if we do not give Him ourselves, it is worthless. If we do not live a life of love, we are nothing.

Growing up is a difficult, wonderful, surprising, fulfilling, disappointing, enlightening, and ultimately defining experience, filled with growing pains, leaving the nest, dissolving dreams, chasing rainbows, tilting at a few windmills, discovering that what we absolutely knew and treasured not long ago is in fact not true, or not important, or both. We see life take us – or those closest to us – to places we did not predict and do not want. At the end, we who are His will find not stuff. We will find Him. He is the destination, the goal, the reason.

In many of our churches, we teach our children and we celebrate their childhood simplicity as we sing "Jesus Loves Me." That is appropriate. As children, we do not see the turns and bumps in the road ahead, and we do not care. We are loved, and that is enough.

The young Solomon was the same way. Blessed with an abundance of wisdom, he saw in everything how he was loved. Read the words of this young one in Song of Songs and in Proverbs, and you cannot help but be struck with an optimism that knows that the way of the wicked leads to destruction because the righteous are loved.

Hopefully, growing up means maturing, becoming less childlike. In turn, it should mean having our focus turn away from ourselves. It is simply no longer enough that we are loved.

What, then, is enough? We work hard, toil, and then we die. The older, even wiser Solomon writes in Ecclesiastes, one of my favorite books in the Bible, that all is empty, all is vain. Everything that was so promising to the more childlike has become a chasing of the wind. Nothing satisfies our soul. None of it gives us meaning or makes us complete. We realize, maybe for the first time, how much we do not know: Where does the wind come from?

Does that make the Proverbs wrong or the Song of Songs irrelevant? Of course not, just as "Jesus Loves Me" is still a critical hymn to each of us. What it does mean is that to the wise, to the mature, to the grown up, to the one honest enough to ask, "How can these things be?", there is something more.

The answer, the something more, is found at the end of Ecclesiastes. To love God is the reason we live. Being loved – even being saved – is the beginning, not the end. The end, the goal, the reason to live is embodied in that first and greatest commandment. The child, as yet unbeckoned by the world, contentedly focuses on "yes, Jesus loves me" and accepts the free grace gift that requires nothing from him. We who know the vanity of the world's call hear the highest call and know that it requires all our heart, all our soul, all our mind, and all our strength.

God does not exercise faith. Faith is the evidence of things not seen, and God sees all. Faith is for us. God has no need for hope, because He who created time and is outside of time has no unknowable future. Hope is ours. But God loves. God is love. Jesus loves me, this I know. You see, to love God is to approach Him, to dare to be like Him. It is time to grow up. For this purpose alone we are made – to love our God.

The heart is the offering we must continue to make as we head to the future. Do justice, but temper it with kindness in a way that the worldly system of so-called justice will never know. Walk with your God on the way to your future, and do so in the humility of knowing that you are the simple, sinful creature allowed to commune with your Creator. With a changed heart, you can then offer your tithes and your time and your actions. Such offerings, like Abel's, will be pleasing to God because you will have already offered what is required of you.

What will our supernatural tax return show? What should we offer? He has shown you, O man, what is good. What does the Lord require of you but to do justice, and to love mercy, and to walk humbly with your God?

To love our God is the reason we live.

Create In Me...

Create in me a clean heart, O God; and renew a right spirit within me. (Psalm 51:10, KJV)

Creation is a holy idea, an idea that we do not spend nearly enough time recognizing or contemplating. Oh sure, we discuss Adam and Eve and whether or not making the universe really took six twenty-four hour periods and what we think about evolution. We make sure that our children understand that God created us and the trees and the birds.

The concept of creation is much more than that simple discussion.

Creation is an ongoing process. The birth of a child reminds us that the Creator is still creating. Springtime renews in us a sense of newness in the world.

In David's anguish at the recognition of his many horrible sins, he cries out with some very human pleas: "Cast me not from thy presence, O Lord. Take not thy Holy Spirit from me." In a calmer time, David knows that God is going to do neither of these things, but it is somehow refreshing to me that even David, the man after God's own heart, could, as I regularly do, forget what is known about God and simply cry out in desperation.

Amid David's despair is a very sound and profound prayer. It is to ask for the creation process once again to take hold of us and make something out of nothing. God is the master of that. Yes, God can take what was dirty and make it clean, but some of us have spent so much time and energy having our present mind, direction, desires, actions, and ideas cleaned up that we feel worn out from the washboard.

Sometimes, we are better off not to ask God to fix what is broken. We are better off leaving our broken lives, destroyed plans, and personal filth behind and have God create in us and for us a completely new, clean heart and life. We need to remember that the one who created the trees and the birds is also the author and finisher of our faith. He is the Creator of each new day, and He regularly creates holy harmony in our hearts and among His people as we break bread together.

Sometimes we want to hold on to part of our old selves. It is more comfortable to ask God to come and pretty up our existing lifestyles so that we can continue in certain ways and attitudes without having a radical shift in anything, and we know that God is faithful to forgive us when we ask. The problem may come in our comfort, as we find that old familiar self pulling us back along familiar paths with sad turns or disasters waiting over the next rise.

God wants more for us than that. He wants better for us than that. He who upholds us with His Spirit wants to remake us, not just clean, but new. He longs to renew us with a right spirit and with joy that we have never even contemplated.

We know that it is out of our heart that our words and actions flow. Take a chance as you approach the Lord. Don't just ask God to help you clean up your words and actions. Ask Him instead to make you a new, clean heart. Experience once again your new creation, where old things are past and all things are become new. Let the Creator create in you.

The Not-Quite-Prodigal And The Quite Holy

We know that God's love is marvelous. The love of God is all the more amazing when we recognize the outstanding biblical characteristic of God – He is holy. Do you remember the moment described in the book of Isaiah when the seraphim appear before the prophet and begin praising God? What is it about God that they emphasize? That's right – it is His holiness. They say that God is "holy, holy, holy." I do not claim to be a Hebrew scholar, but I do understand that the way the Hebrew language provides extra emphasis is to repeat. In English, we might say that God is "very, very holy." Not in Hebrew. Instead, that language would use its words to say "holy, holy, holy." The nature of God – perfect, good, holy – and the nature of sinners are mutually exclusive. His very being is not able to abide the presence of sin.

Notice, nowhere else in scripture is this technique used. God is not described as "mercy, mercy, mercy." No prophet calls Him "faithful, faithful, faithful." He is not ever described as "love, love, love."

But He is holy. He is holy, holy, holy. I think we are intended to notice that.

What does it mean to be holy? Well, it first means pure. God is not like us, with our sins and our mistakes. God is perfect, sinless, unstained. Saying that is insufficient though, because holiness goes beyond what He is not. God is. God is holy. Being holy means that God is set apart. He is unique.

Holiness is the defining feature of God, and it is the holiness of God that makes our sin such a problem. Did you ever stop to think why the wages of sin is death? It is because everlasting life in the presence of God is possible only if we are, like God, holy.

Who shall ascend into the hill of the LORD? Or who shall stand in his holy place? He that hath clean hands, and a pure heart; who hath not lifted up his soul unto vanity, nor sworn deceitfully. He shall receive the blessing from the LORD, and righteousness from the God of his salvation. (Psalm 24:3-5, KJV)

To remain pure, the perfect one cannot come into contact with sin. If a small clot of dirt is thrown into perfectly pure water, the whole basin becomes cloudy and muddy. To live with God forever, we must be as pure as He. He cannot commune with us otherwise. His holiness will not allow it. To ascend to live with Him, we must have clean hands.

That creates quite a problem! Because we all – you, you, you, and I – sin. Every last one of us is stained by our own choices, our own decisions, our own failures, our own mistakes. I know that some disagree, thinking that the saved have achieved perfection – or at least sinlessness – because Jesus has come into their hearts. I respectfully differ. We can take up a philosophical argument about original sin and about whether we could avoid sin, but that debate is sophistry because we all sin. Whether we could theoretically help it or not, we are all sinners. That means we are impure, unholy, imperfect, stained beings who cannot spend eternity with God.

In the law, we use a phrase to describe those who are not entitled to equitable relief from the court – we say they have "unclean hands." In life, that applies to all of us – we have unclean hands, we have impure hearts, and we may not stand in His holy place.

That thought can be quite a downer. The wages of sin is death, both because sin is violative of God's very nature and because He can only spend eternity with those unstained by sin. Yes, God is holy.

Fortunately, God is also love… and mercy… and forgiveness. It is with these attributes in mind that we join David in Psalm 51, to say, "Have mercy," and to beg forgiveness. David voiced this plea when he realized the mess he had made of his life. You know the story of David and Bathsheba. What started with avoiding his royal duties and a simple invasion of privacy escalated through lust and adultery to lying and murder… and not just one murder. In order to make sure that Bathsheba's husband Uriah died, David condemned an entire squadron of his troops to unnecessary and cruel death. Now, for the first time, what David has done has become real to him.

The emotion of the fifty-first Psalm should not be lost on any of us. We have all cried out in the darkness, "Lord, have mercy!"

Those of us who are Christians have all lived through those dark nights of the soul to realize that we are still, despite our sin and our pleas for mercy, His children. His salvation is never taken away from us; and yet, we are not the same as we were before we recognized that sin.

The miracle, of course, is that God does have mercy on us and does restore us. Despite our unclean hands, He brings us mercy and pardon and salvation. The wonder of the cross is that the stain, the impurity, the mud of sin was taken from us by our savior so that we can commune with our holy God. I cannot explain that to you, but I believe it with my life. The wages of sin is still death, and God's justice certainly demands that the wages be paid. Someone has to die.

Before we can have a relationship with Him, before we can be called children of God, before we can escape the slavery of evil darkness, we must be freed from the bonds of sin. Something has to happen to make us like God – perfect, holy, good. That something is forgiveness. The mercy and love of God have provided that the wages, owed by us, were paid once and for all by another.

My late friend Grant Cunningham wrote a beautiful song called "The Great Divide" recorded by Point of Grace, in which the chorus says, "There is a bridge to cross the great divide." It is a divide between us and God caused by our own sin, and the work of Jesus has been to build that bridge. As Grant's song so cleverly puts it later, "There is a cross to bridge the great divide."

That brings us to the magic of this story:

Jesus continued: "There was a man who had two sons. The younger one said to his father, 'Father, give me my share of the estate.' So he divided his property between them. "Not long after that, the younger son got together all he had, set off for a distant country and there squandered his wealth in wild living. After he had spent everything, there was a severe famine in that whole country, and he began to be in need. So he went and hired himself out to a citizen of that country, who sent him to his fields to feed pigs. He longed to fill his stomach with the pods that the pigs were eating, but no one gave him anything. When he came to his senses, he said, 'How many of my father's hired men have food to spare, and here I am starving to death! I will set out and go back to my father and say to him: Father, I have sinned against heaven and against you. I am no longer worthy to be called your son; make me like one of your hired men.' So he got up and went to his father.

"But while he was still a long way off, his father saw him and was filled with compassion for him; he ran to his son, threw his arms around him and kissed him. The son said to him, 'Father, I have sinned against heaven and against you. I am no longer worthy to be called your son.' But the father said to his servants, 'Quick! Bring the best robe and put it on him. Put a ring on his finger and sandals on his feet. Bring the fattened calf and kill it. Let's have a feast and celebrate. For this son of mine was dead and is alive again; he was lost and is found.' So they began to celebrate.

"Meanwhile, the older son was in the field. When he came near the house, he heard music and dancing. So he called one of the servants and

asked him what was going on. 'Your brother has come,' he replied, 'and your father has killed the fattened calf because he has him back safe and sound.' The older brother became angry and refused to go in. So his father went out and pleaded with him. But he answered his father, 'Look! All these years I've been slaving for you and never disobeyed your orders. Yet you never gave me even a young goat so I could celebrate with my friends. But when this son of yours who has squandered your property with prostitutes comes home, you kill the fattened calf for him!' 'My son,' the father said, 'you are always with me, and everything I have is yours. But we had to celebrate and be glad, because this brother of yours was dead and is alive again; he was lost and is found.'" (Luke 15:11-32, NIV)

I can just imagine. Christ is sitting among would-be friends and followers. He knows them in fact to be skeptics, critics, and enemies. There are undoubtedly some lawyers in the bunch! He begins to weave this story of a certain man with two sons. You see, if ever there was a story with which any audience could relate, it is this one. We have all left home seeking what we thought was the good life, only to find ourselves in a pig sty of our own making. If you have not awakened there yet, then count your blessings. You have been protected from yourself. *Prodigal* means "wastefully and recklessly extravagant." We are all prodigal with what the Father has freely given us.

Picture Jesus telling this story. Can you put yourself in the audience? Can you feel your innermost soul wanting to call out "Have mercy!" You do not, of course, you stop short You tell yourself that you are not, after all, in a pig sty. You are still able to save yourself. You just need to act a little better. You are just certain that you can and that you will. If that is you, I want you to pay special attention. Perhaps you are the "not-quite-Prodigal."

I had a youth minister who preached three sermons on this story, his favorite parable. He called them (not terribly imaginatively) "Prodigal Son," "The Waiting Father," and "The Older Brother." The first version is how the story is most often preached. We wander far from home and tread the paths of sin, and then we desire to come home. Good story, life changing. You know it by heart. It does not ever seem to change you much, but you surely tell it well.

The second story, that of the waiting Father, is also one that you can fire off rapidly. You love to tell of how His love, excelling the loves of all others, waits with open arms when we shed bitter, penitential tears. We Christians tend to wallow in forgiveness, and we are genuinely thankful for His grace and for the indescribably wide mercy He shows us. Once more, coming home is a joyous, thrilling event to talk about. Once more, we not-quite-Prodigals repeat the same patterns, so that we continue to require grace and mercy, since we deserve so much less (or so much more, depending how you look at it).

The third view of the story is one the not-quite-Prodigals often choose to ignore. You see, the older brother resembles most of us on a daily basis when we are not reveling in the muck. Instead, daily, we are just having a passing romance with junk (muck is such an ugly word for us not-quite-Prodigals) that we know, deep down, we will leave when we have had enough. We tell ourselves that we are not like the older brother, and indeed we are not when we are honestly repentant and truly seeking to return to obedience. Unfortunately, that true repentance does not happen nearly as often as we not-quite-Prodigals pretend, does it?

Stay with me, all you not-quite-Prodigals. Keep up, all of you who can think of twenty people off the top of your head who are a lot worse sinners than you are. I am writing to you, especially if you are a full-fledged member of a church.

I think that it is hardest to come home when we think we never left. We look around us and see the same walls, fellowship with the same people, go through the same routines, speak the same words, go through the same motions, and make the same noises that we always have; why then should we need to return? For that matter, why should we even care when others come back, after they have wasted all that the Father has provided? We might even question their sincerity in rededication and doubt that they have truly come home.

The answer lies, once again, in scripture and in the heart of Christ. Home is not a place. Home is not an address or a geographical point of latitude and longitude. Home is where the Father is, where He says "My child, you are always with me, and all that I have is yours." We look around to see how much kingdom we have enjoyed today, and we suddenly are faced with the reality that we do not have to go anywhere to leave home.

Neil Diamond sings that "Home is the most excellent place of all." How right he is. Home is with the Father, where His arms of love are open wide, outstretched and waiting, where all that is His is ours.

So where does that leave us?

First, we know that we are sinners. Maybe you are every bit the Prodigal Son. You have taken the good gifts of the Father and squandered them and ruined your life, and you feel that you are worth nothing and that you should remain among the outcast and overlooked of society. You are staring at that

Great Divide, and you know that you have caused it. Tearfully, you realize that you cannot see across it.

Or maybe you are a not-quite-Prodigal. Yes, you will admit, at least to yourself, that you are a sinner, that you have fallen short of the glorious plan that God has for you, but you are so much better than those around you. You simply cannot admit that you need to come home... but... you know... and God knows.

Second, we know that God is holy, perfect, pure. That means that we, as sinners, cannot live with God. Our sin has created a chasm – the great divide – between us and God that we are powerless to bridge. We have unclean hands and cannot ascend to the hill of the Lord. We cannot stand in His holy place. In the darkness, when nobody else is there, we come face to face with our failures and have no choice but to cry out, "Oh God, have mercy on me!"

That brings us to the third, wonderful point. Christ has forgiven us. The bridge between us and God over the canyon created by our sins – the debt we owed that we could not pay – has been built when Christ chose to pay a debt He did not owe. The lawyer in me cannot prove to you the metes and bounds of the way it was done, nor can I provide an expert witness to explain to you how He did that, but the believer in me can point to a place called Calvary where He did it. There is a bridge to cross the great divide. There is a cross to bridge that great divide.

When we pray the prayer seeking mercy, we hear the One who is standing on the road eagerly waiting for us to turn around, call, "Oh sinner, come home!" The marvelous grace of our loving, holy Lord exceeds our sin and our guilt, and we can run once again into His open arms.

Let the older brother in you rejoice for those returning from the pig sty, but do not forget to bring the older brother in your home. After all, home is the most excellent place of all.

Running with the Horses

My favorite hymn – one that I want sung at my funeral, among other places – is "It Is Well with My Soul." Written by a lawyer! Its composition followed the discovery that all four of his children had drowned in a shipwreck while crossing the ocean to meet him. The lyrics arise out of his struggle with grief and anger and all of the emotions that come with a moment like that. The hymn concludes with the writer's ability to understand the comfort of God enough to say, "Though Satan should buffet, though trials should come, let this blest assurance control: that Christ has regarded my helpless estate.... It is well."

I think that experiencing the comfort of God has to be a part, if not the central tenet, of the testimony that most of us have to offer. That does not mean that all of us have faced the tragic death of even one of our own children. Thankfully, I have not had to face that pain.

It does mean that we live in a world where bad things happen. God's comfort is necessary because we are uncomfortable, battered, sick, sore, grieved, alone, abandoned, or desperate. I have seen clients go bankrupt. I have seen partners, clients, and my own company lose trials worth millions of dollars. I have seen colleagues belittled to their face.

But what I have seen as a lawyer pales in comparison to what life has shown me elsewhere. I have sat in the hospital with my very sick child. I have seen my own dreams dashed. I have waited through my mother's cancer surgery. I have attended my father-in-law's funeral.

I am one of the lucky ones though. I have not had to face a fraction what many of you face right now.

I do not think there is a person on this earth who has not grappled with the questions that arise when we see reality. God is all-powerful, so He could have stopped that bad thing. God is all-loving, so He must have wanted to stop that bad thing. God is all-knowing, so He must have known that the bad thing was happening. Yet, despite His knowledge and His love and His power, the bad thing still happens. We cry, and maybe we get mad and shake a fist at heaven, or maybe we just shrug our shoulders and decide that God is not nearly as interested as He was back in biblical days when He always seemed to be appearing to folks and healing their leprosy.

So, why do bad things happen to good Christians? I have some answers for that, but I cannot promise that they will satisfy you. I also cannot promise to cover them sufficiently in this space. Perhaps that is another book.

The first answer is that there is no answer for every tragedy because we live in a fallen world. This is a world where bad things simply happen, often with no apparent or satisfying explanation. For me, the question, "Why do bad things happen to good Christians" assumes that Christians are entitled to some special shield from the rain and the shipwrecks. I choose to look at the question of "Why" this way – "Why not?" Who better to receive and endure what life has to offer than those who are gifted with the Holy Spirit and who know the comfort of God?

I know that does not provide much of an answer to you when it is your child lying under the oxygen tent. Believe me, Gena and I were there in the fall of 1996 while our four-month-old Carolyn struggled to breathe under the watchful eyes of the Vanderbilt Children's Hospital staff. I think it is part of God's answer nonetheless to know that Christians are the ones best equipped to handle life's dangers and struggles.

There is no question that pain, evil, and suffering are bad. I do not believe that God sends them or allows them just to make us value other things more. I do believe, however, that we should – indeed we must – look beyond the evil to see the wonders of our God. Seeing the black in the picture makes the colors brighter; honoring the rest in the symphony makes the crescendos more musical; not choosing to take the wide road makes the narrow way more victorious. God is a brilliant craftsman, artist, composer, and director; His gifts are perfect. Our loving and omniscient God has created this world for us, Christians are not exempt from all it has to offer.

Second, I believe in a real devil, a very active Satan who is working evil in this world. One reason that bad things happen is because there is a powerful force for bad that has a foothold in our world. Jesus discusses him throughout the gospels, and the prince of this world is still possessing, foiling, seducing, and corrupting God's creations.

Third, we may not always know what is bad. This is a hard lesson for litigators to learn. Too often we are sure what a case is "worth," and then a jury surprises us by bringing back a verdict that is a small fraction of what we predicted or orders of magnitude greater than the worst we feared. What that tells us lawyers is that we have lost perspective on what the real world thinks is good and bad and valuable and worthless.

It is the same thing with our human perspective of what is good and bad. We do not have the eyes or the perspective of the Everlasting One, and it borders on arrogance for us puny humans to declare that we know everything about what is good. I believe that there are things that happen that are absolutely for the best in the big picture. The problem is that we have no concept of the big picture. In the words of a wise student in a Sunday School class I taught, God is continually creating, painting, and perfecting a huge mosaic, and even with scripture, prayer, and experience, we see only a small corner. Our view makes certain things appear certain ways, and we call them "good" or "bad." From a heavenly viewpoint, those events may be good, bad, or neither.

I know that also does not answer many of the questions, and there are some things that are bound to be bad from any perspective. I do not believe that God thinks it is good when the four-year-old is killed by a drunk driver. Still, I do think that there are many times that we have no idea what the "good" result might be.

A fourth answer is that sometimes God sends or allows calamity because we deserve it. I am not a proponent of the theory that we serve a wrathful, vengeful God hurling thunderbolts and conjuring up new diseases or ordering terrorists around in order to punish the popular sin of the week. On the other hand, I do not believe you can read scripture honestly without recognizing that God disciplines those He loves and that He punishes the evil.

Fifth is perhaps the toughest to accept but the deepest and most meaningful of the answers. It is found in the prophecy of Jeremiah:

Righteous art Thou, O Lord, that I would plead my case with Thee;
Indeed I would discuss matters of justice with Thee:
Why has the way of the wicked prospered?
Why are all those who deal in treachery at ease?
Thou hast planted them, they have also taken root;
They grow, they have even produced fruit.
Thou art near to their lips
But far from their mind.
But Thou knowest me, O Lord;
Thou seest me;
And Thou dost examine my heart's attitude toward Thee.
Drag them off like sheep for the slaughter
And set them apart for a day of carnage!
How long is the land to mourn
And the vegetation of the countryside to wither?
For the wickedness of those who dwell in it,

Animals and birds have been snatched away,
Because men have said, "He will not see our latter ending."
"If you have run with footmen and they have tired you out, then how can
you compete with horses?
If you fall down in a land of peace, how will you do in the thicket of the
Jordan?" (Jeremiah 12:1-5, NAS)

If you have grown tired running with the footmen, then how will you ever run with the horses? You have to face and conquer the problems that come to you now, in a land of peace, so that you have some chance of victory when you face the swelling of the Jordan. If you did not recognize it, Jeremiah's words are Hebrew for "when the going gets tough, the tough get going."

Don't you see? God wants us to run with the horses. He desires for us to mount up with wings as eagles. God's plan is for us to walk on water.

We cannot automatically and immediately run with the horses. We are not the gold that we need to be until we have first gone through a refiner's fire, where impurities and weaknesses are removed and only the finest and most valuable to the Kingdom remains.

It was the Apostle Paul who wrote that we all must suffer if we are to be joint heirs with Christ. We join in His suffering so that we can be glorified together with Him. I do not understand that, and I do not welcome it, but I believe it. You may well know real suffering right now. Maybe it is in your body or in your family. Perhaps your business or your farm is in such a state that you are truly experiencing travail. If not now, you will know it in your life, if you are lucky enough to live that long.

That is where the comfort of God comes in. There is no question that bad things happen in this fallen world. At least they are bad as far as we can figure. The fact that those happenings may be coloring our world so that tomorrow will be brighter does not help, for the moment. The idea that an evil person is being punished or a good person is being disciplined is irrelevant to us as we experience what seems like yet another crushing blow. As even more lightning seems to strike us, the thought of being able to run with the horses sometime in the future could not matter less to us.

How fortunate that we serve a God who does not leave us there! He, as He always does, seeks us out. He comes to us. At Christmas time, we call His coming "advent." In truth, advent happens repeatedly – our God seeks us and finds us and comes to us.

Before we can run with the horses, we need once again to welcome and to wait upon Him. For the prophet, advent was the explanation of the ultimate comfort of God, as he penned in one single chapter these amazing words of comfort:

"Comfort, O comfort My people," says your God... "Let every valley be lifted up, and every mountain and hill be made low; and let the rough ground become a plain, and the rugged terrain a broad valley; then the glory of the Lord will be revealed, and all flesh will see it together; for the mouth of the Lord has spoken."... The grass withers, the flower fades, but the word of our God stands forever. Get yourself up on a high mountain, O Zion, bearer of good news, lift up your voice mightily, O Jerusalem, bearer of good news; lift it up, do not fear. Say to the cities of Judah, "Here is your God!"... Like a shepherd He will tend His flock, in His arm He will gather the lambs, and carry them in His bosom.... Do you not know? Have you not heard? The Everlasting God, the Lord, the Creator of the ends of the earth does not become weary or tired. His understanding is inscrutable. He gives strength to the weary, and to him who lacks might He increases power. Though youths grow weary and tired, and vigorous young men stumble badly, yet those who wait for the Lord will gain new strength; they will mount up with wings like eagles, they will run and not get tired, they will walk and not become weary. (Isaiah 40, selected verses, NAS)

When advent happens – when we truly wait on Him and begin to understand what it is to mount up with wings as eagles – we finally understand about running with the horses.

It is then that the comfort of God takes over. We stop asking why bad things happen and start resolving to move forward despite the bad things. Then the colors of the great mosaic sparkle brightly around the black that has been recently painted. Then, when we have waited for the Lord and been renewed with His strength, we are ready to run with the horses.

Abundant Life

As the chair of my law firm's recruiting committee, I talked to a number of law students wanting a job. I frequently asked them why they chose to go to law school, and the typical response echoed what I said myself years ago – something about helping others with their problems and making the world a better place. Some of them were very sincere – I certainly thought I meant it! For many others, though, a career in law was the goal solely because it held out the promise of money, respect, and a powerful place in society.

Most people choose this career because of the advantages they think it will bring to their life. Few of them would use the term "abundant life" to describe that goal, because they are biblically illiterate if for no other reason, but it does describe what they want. They just do not all know it.

Think with me for a moment about one of the most misunderstood verses in scripture. You probably know it well. It is Jesus talking: "I have come that they might have life and have it more abundantly." (John 10:10, KJV)

I won't say that is the most misunderstood verse. I'll reserve that title for the verses about handling snakes or the number 144,000, but I do think a lot of people misunderstand these words of Christ. We act as if we think "life more abundantly" is the same thing as living problem-free. Then the problems come, and we wonder why the "abundance" has left us.

One of my earliest country music memories is hearing Lynn Anderson sing, "I beg your pardon; I never promised you a rose garden." Somehow, we tend to a candy store theology that teaches that if we say the right prayers and give the right offering we can push a button and get exactly what we want and that nothing bad will happen to us. I have read the words of a sports hero who survived a car accident because, he says, while the car was hurtling through the air he took his hands off the wheel and called out the name of Jesus.

Most Christians who have lived in the same world I have for about fifteen minutes will tell you that such theology is all wrong. God never promised us a rose garden. God did not keep the rain from falling on Noah. He did not shut down Nebuchadnezzar's fiery furnace. He did not close the mouths of Nero's lions. He did not keep Parkinson's disease from Billy Graham. He did not keep lung cancer from my non-smoking, church-going father-in-law. Even Lazarus, after the Master had raised him from the grave, died again. I think the wide receiver I mentioned in the last paragraph might want to revisit his Bible – one rather famous character in that book went to a garden to pray, calling on the name of God to prevent catastrophe. He was crucified the next day.

There is no question that we live in a world where we are not exempt from what Dr. Seuss calls bang-ups and hang-ups. We find ourselves in slumps, just like anybody else. The very apostles of Christ found themselves tossed by the wind and the waves, and the storm was not immediately calmed, even when Jesus saw their plight. The rose garden theologians cannot deal with that reality. They just continue to preach that if you do what they say, your children will be perfect, you will have lots of money, and your chili will win the cook-off competition – all bad things will go away.

That is the catch – the rose garden crowd preaches about what can be taken away.

Our theology cannot be based on what is subtracted from life. We are offered abundant life. My dictionary says *abundant* means "bountiful, ample, generous." We who seek first the kingdom of God are promised that "all these things will be added" to our lives. Instead of running a candy store and preventing the rain, ours is a God who sends arks for the rain, who takes our loaves and fishes and feeds thousands, and who brings us out of those fiery furnaces to see the next day. He is a God who, although He does not always choose to calm the storms, calms His children amidst the storms and then calls for us to walk on the water among the very same waves that seconds before were threatening our existence. That is abundant life.

There are faithful Christians who believe that my definition of "abundance" is utopian. They tell me that the best we can hope for is to find a place to walk despite the waves. They preach that Jesus teaches us how to swim better. I do not disagree, for I believe that Jesus does empower us to thrive despite what the world throws at us. But I believe there is more. I believe the "life more abundantly" that the Father has in mind for us is what the world would call miraculous. I believe the lesson from Peter's walking on the water is that you and I can walk on water. I believe the lesson from David's slingshot story is that we can slay giants. I believe the lesson from the story of Zaccheus is that we can overcome even our own failures. I believe the lesson of Jesus' words about faith as small as a mustard seed is that the power to move mountains is within our grasp.

Being a Christian does not guarantee that you will learn the right words to yell out so you can survive car wrecks or that you will be in a position to make the world a better place through your career, nor does it do much to help you become rich, powerful, and famous - even if you are a Christian lawyer.

The rains will fall. I beg your pardon, but Christian or not, you will get sick. The neighbor's dog will still bite you. But through it all, Christ has come to give you life more abundantly.

As Dr. Seuss would say, "Your mountain is waiting. So get on your way!"

Finding a Crown for God on a Really Bad Day

O God, why hast Thou rejected us forever?
Why does Thine anger smoke against the sheep of Thy pasture?...
Thine adversaries have roared in the midst of Thy meeting place;
They have set up their own standards for signs.
It seems as if one had lifted up
His axe in a forest of trees.
And now all its carved work
They smash with hatchet and hammers.
They have burned Thy sanctuary to the ground;
They have defiled the dwelling place of Thy name.
They said in their heart, "Let us completely subdue them."
They have burned all the meeting places of God in the land.
We do not see our signs;
There is no longer any prophet,
Nor is there any among us who knows how long.
How long, O God, will the adversary revile,
And the enemy spurn Thy name forever?
Why dost Thou withdraw Thy hand, even Thy right hand?
From within Thy bosom, destroy them!
Yet God is my king ... (Psalm 74:1-12, NAS)

But the fruit of the Spirit is love, joy, peace, patience, kindness, goodness,
faithfulness, gentleness and self-control. (Galatians 5:22-23, NIV)

"Crown Him with Many Crowns" is a hymn we have sung repeatedly and joyously out of feelings of abundance, happiness, and easy praise for the one who provides for our every need. This song springs from a soul enlivened with the provisions of God.

I remember with as much clarity as sadness a day in which my life had more chaos than we ought to have to face. Those who have experienced the gut-wrenching turmoil of watching your wife be told she has just miscarried know what I mean: the awful combination of watching your true love's world explode even as you have yourself lost the hope embodied by what was alive just yesterday in her womb.

When that happened, I did not feel like crowning anybody. Come to think of it, there are lots of days when I don't feel like it. But it is not just me. Let me turn the focus away from me; I want to tell you a true story about a friend of mine – for now I will call her Pam. Pam and I grew up together. Her parents and my parents were and are best friends. She grew up and married a doctor in a small town near Nashville. Several years ago, Pam's husband was involved in a tragic situation in which a girl he was treating died. He was sued for malpractice, and I had the privilege of representing him. He won, but the trial and the accusations left indelible marks on this very good man.

Then, a few years later, on September 11 no less, their seventeen-year-old daughter was killed by a drunk driver.

After the malpractice trial, they moved to the Gulf coast. One tragic late August day in 2005, there was a picture in the paper of their ten-year-old son watching their house float away in the aftermath of Hurricane Katrina. They were left with only the clothes on their back. What they lost included pictures of their recently deceased daughter. Her sister's email to me said that Pam did not know what to pray for.

It does not seem to stop. Less than two years later, the very week I am writing these words, Pam's sister has lost her own son and her husband to yet another drunk driver.

It is not just Pam, of course. Most of us have an aunt, a brother, or a friend profoundly affected by a hurricane, or by war, or by disease. In fact most of us have been affected personally. It is Tsunami, or 9/11, or hundreds of thousands of victims of Saddam Hussein, or millions of victims of Pol Pot or Stalin or Hitler or Ceaucescu. It is the hundreds of thousands for whom the highways have meant tragedy, many at the hands of cruel recklessness and intoxication.

We are Christians, so we accept that God is on His throne. We have some form of an answer as to why bad things happen, and we accept. Except that scripture – like our many hymns – does not just call us to accept, it calls us to praise.

Of course, our praise does not depend on how we feel. But I still do not understand how Pam was supposed to praise as she grieved over her daughter and saw the house floating away.

Just as praise is not dependent on my feelings, it is also not dependent on my understanding. It is OK that I do not understand how victims of life are supposed to praise, so long as I do not fail to praise. I am to trust in the Lord with all my heart and lean not on my own understanding.

So I read this: "Why are you downcast, O my soul? Why so disturbed within me? Put your hope in God, for I will yet praise him." (Psalm 42:5, NIV) And I read this: "Deep calls to deep in the roar of your waterfalls; all your waves and breakers have swept over me. I say to God my Rock, 'Why have you forgotten me? Why must I go about mourning, oppressed by the enemy?' My bones suffer mortal agony as my foes taunt me, saying to me all day long, 'Where is your God?' Why are you downcast, O my soul? Why so disturbed within me? Put your hope in God, for I will yet praise him." (Psalm 42:7-11, NIV)

I remember Sunday, September 16, 2001, the first Sunday after the World Trade Center attacks, when my pastor preached about finding a way to praise in the aftermath. He noted that, since he did not know how to praise at that moment either, he looked to the Psalms. There, David, in his moments of worst grief, went back to basics, even basing an entire Psalm on a simple acrostic made by the Hebrew alphabet. Sometimes, we have to go back to our ABCs. We do not understand it all; we simply cling to this basic, found in another Psalm:

The Lord is my shepherd. I shall not want. He maketh me to lie down in green pastures. He leadeth me beside the still waters. He restoreth my soul. He leadeth me in paths of righteousness for his name's sake. Yea, though I walk through the valley of the shadow of death, I will fear no evil, for thou art with me; thy rod and thy staff, they comfort me. Thou preparest a table before me in the presence of my enemies. Thou anointest my head with oil; my cup overflows. Surely goodness and mercy will follow me all the days of my life, and I will dwell in the house of the LORD forever. (Psalm 23, KJV)

The fruit of the Spirit, like our call to praise, has nothing to do with our feelings. Although we are unhappy, the joy of His victory is within us. Despite the turmoil and the storms that surround us, peace of His assurance flows through us. When we do not have a nice bone in our bodies, kindness – His kindness – emanates from us.

Put another way, when He is our lord and His Spirit bears fruit within us and about us, the dirges and melancholy tunes we would play are drowned by the music of heavenly anthems.

Lord, you have been our dwelling place throughout all generations. Before the mountains were born or you brought forth the earth and the world, from everlasting to everlasting you are God. You turn men back to dust, saying, "Return to dust, O sons of men." For a thousand years in your sight are like a day that has just gone by, or like a watch in the night.... Who knows the power of your anger? For your wrath is as great as the fear that is due you. Teach us to number our days aright, that we may gain a heart of wisdom. Relent, O LORD! How long will it be? Have compassion on your servants. Satisfy us in the morning with your unfailing love, that we may sing for joy and be glad all our days. Make us glad for as many days as you have afflicted us, for as many years as we have seen trouble. May your deeds be shown to your servants, your splendor to their children. May the favor of the Lord our God rest upon us; establish the work of our hands for us— yes, establish the work of our hands. (Psalm 90:1-4, 11-17, NIV)

The conflicting emotions of Psalm 90 mirror our lives. In the mention of the travail of the world found in verses 5 -10 (the part I left out of the previous passage), we get a hint of the context:

You sweep men away in the sleep of death; they are like the new grass of the morning— though in the morning it springs up new, by evening it is dry and withered. We are consumed by your anger and terrified by your indignation. You have set our iniquities before you, our secret sins in the light of your presence. All our days pass away under your wrath; we finish our years with a moan. The length of our days is seventy years— or eighty, if we have the strength; yet their span is but trouble and sorrow, for they quickly pass, and we fly away. (Psalm 90:5-10, NIV)

I think the Psalmist must have been having a day like Pam had, or Gena and I have had, or you have had when he wrote this. He must have seen the wonder of new life and the promise and hope it brings, only to turn around and be faced with the reality of disease, suffering, and death. He must have been, like us, confused and frustrated, and maybe a little bit angry. biblical scholars believe that Moses is the writer here, and I bet he wrote it on a really bad day in the desert, maybe after about thirty-seven years of wandering.

It is in these times that perspective is the most important and yet the hardest to achieve. How are we satisfied? How can the morning see us sing for joy? Who can be glad?

You see, our perspective is limited by our humanity, by our weakness, by our selfishness, by our time. We find ourselves leaning on our own understanding. We see only our own generation. We see a month, a day, a moment.

Despite his momentary feelings, the Psalmist begins by recognizing that, fortunately, our faith is not dependent on the ebb and flow of our emotions. Our God is our refuge, our mighty fortress. He is from generation to generation, and a thousand years are as a simple yesterday to the one who is from everlasting to everlasting. He was God before the mountains were brought forth and before

36

even the earth was created. He is bigger than our doubts and bigger than our hurts and bigger than even our deaths. That is what eternal life is all about. He has us firmly established. His hand is on us, even as we are caught in the many devastating storms that life includes.

This God is ours. We hold him in our earthly lives, so we are troubled on every side, but not distressed; perplexed, but not in despair; persecuted, but not forsaken; cast down, but not destroyed.

Our perspective must not only allow us to see that our present hurt will not conquer us; our perspective must rise to see the hurt and the storms of our fellow man. We are called above our own tumult to follow Christ as He steps into the stormy sea. We are called to live for Him even as we see suffering and loss in our own lives.

From where does this perspective come? Sometimes, it comes from stepping back and seeing that God is God. He always has been and always will be... from age to age. It comes from seeing once again, as if anew, His awesome deeds. Remember, what marvelous miracles happen to His people! It comes from seeing through the eyes of our children the sheer majesty of God. Our moment, the pain of which is undeniably real, nonetheless shrinks in perspective to His master plan, to His reign, to His glory.

We pray for healing, for relief, for change. Even Jesus asked for the cup to be taken from Him. Then we step back as we gain a glimpse of His perspective, and we join our Lord in affirming "nevertheless, not my will but Thine be done."

We do not always understand, but we do not have to. "Thou art God." That has been enough from age to age. "Thou art God."

On those awful days, I may be able to crown Him as Savior. Maybe we can conjure up a crown for Him as Creator, but crowning Him with the many crowns to which He is entitled is difficult.

In the face of death, loss, and discouragement, the fruit of the Spirit is peace, patience, faithfulness, and self-control. We lose that which is corruptible, but we have gained that which is incorruptible. Behold His hands and side! He has not promised us that we shall always be happy. He has promised us eternal life, the joy and peace of His Spirit, and the assurance that we are not alone. He has promised us that His glory shall not end. Even, then, amid death and loss, we crown Him the lord of life.

In the face of despair, emptiness, and confusion, the fruit of the Spirit is joy, love, goodness, and kindness. We are set apart as a chosen people, a royal priesthood, and a holy nation to show forth His praises, despite what we may feel at the time. In light of His victorious resurrection, our strife, while so very real, is not overwhelming, because He has died for us. He is our matchless king. Notwithstanding our grief, our failures, and those things that are not to be, we crown Him the Lord of love.

"Crown Him with Many Crowns" is one of those hymns that enable us to praise when we don't feel like it. That song means more to me, today, not when it is sung out of response to abundant provision but when it is sung as fruit of His Spirit in me, the one Spirit who gives many gifts to us even when the world is taken away from us. It is times when we are downcast, discouraged, and without life, that we awaken our souls and sing of Him who died for us.

What crown do you need to bestow upon Him today? Is it the crown of love? Is it the crown of peace? Is it the crown of salvation? If your week has been good, crown Him the lord of life. If you have had a week like the ones we have all had, remember that He is on His throne. Hail your Redeemer who has died for you. Crown Him with many crowns.

Fear Not?

But Jesus immediately said to them: "Take courage! It is I. Don't be afraid." (Matthew 14:27, NIV)

Fear is a very natural thing. That can be a problem, because we learn scripture verses with words like "Don't be afraid." We sing "Because He lives, all fear is gone."

It is a truth of life that nobody can ever prevent all of the bad things that could happen. That is a sad truth to my clients. Despite their best efforts, something has happened to them that requires a lawyer. Perhaps my client is a doctor who was unable to save a life and now finds herself sued by a distraught parent. Maybe it is the old man whose insurance is not paying a medical bill. Or it is my friend who is self-employed and who is owed money by another lawyer who will not pay her. Despite my best efforts, there is not always something I can do to make it OK. Sometimes, I can "fix it," but oftentimes the lawsuit comes anyway, or the insurance company still refuses to pay. Then my clients know real fear.

For my colleagues on the criminal law side, of course, fear is a daily experience for their clients, because they are not facing just lawsuits or unpaid bills – they fear that they are going to jail, or worse.

Having a lawyer does not make those things go away, just as having the world's best doctor does not keep you from getting sick, and watching the best meteorologist in town does not stop the tornado.

Somehow, though, we want religion to fix everything. Instead of looking for peace through the storm and strength to withstand the attacks of this world, we tend to demand a savior who will lift us out of this life so that we have nothing to fear. We don't want abundance ("life plus"); we want subtraction ("life minus"). We want all the unpleasantness, conflict, and trials simply to go away.

It is undeniable, despite the fact that Christ lives, that all fear is not gone. The Christian wife may fear her abusive husband. The alcoholic Christian may fear his own actions. You may fear for your job. A young man I know who is dying of AIDS faces fears I cannot begin to imagine.

Despite our best actions, our strong faith, and our fervent prayers, the waters still rise into floods, or we see no alternative but fire before us. We do not see the presence of God or feel His power, and we fear.

What, then, do words like "Fear not" have to say to us?

They say that those things which we humans naturally fear are in fact not too big for God. We know that in the mystery of God there is a plan for us, just as He had a plan for His people when He first said:

> "Do not fear, for I have redeemed you; I have called you by name; you are Mine! "When you pass through the waters, I will be with you; and through the rivers, they will not overflow you. When you walk through the fire, you will not be scorched, nor will the flame burn you." (Isaiah 43:1-2, NAS)

When we pass through the waters, God is with us, and suddenly, as long as our eyes are on Him, we find ourselves walking on the water.

The floods come, often caused by life's storms, and we fear when we realize that He has not calmed the storm or held back the flood. Then, with eyes on Him, we realize the flood is not sweeping over us.

God does not prevent our walk from passing through the fires of life; we smell smoke, and the fears come. Then we turn our gaze on the one who is in the fire with us, and we know that we will not be consumed.

Noah was not saved from the flood. He was saved in the flood. The faith of Shadrach, Meshach, and Abednego did not keep them from the fiery furnace, but it kept them through the fiery furnace.

Our God, who loves us with an everlasting love, counts the very hairs on our heads and calls us each, individually, by name. We are precious in His sight, and nothing can snatch us from His hand.

> But now be strong, O Zerubbabel,' declares the LORD. 'Be strong, O Joshua son of Jehozadak, the high priest. Be strong, all you people of the land,' declares the LORD, 'and work. For I am with you,' declares the LORD Almighty. 'This is what I covenanted with you when you came out of Egypt. And my Spirit remains among you. Do not fear.' (Haggai 2:4-5, NIV)

> Do not be terrified; do not be discouraged, for the LORD your God will be with you wherever you go. (Joshua 1:9, NIV)

These promises can be misconstrued and taken out of context. When we do that, we can easily be led to disappointments, crises of faith, and false hopes. After all, none of us has a path free from snares, and we are clearly not protected from all the problems of life. (Let's not, however, be guilty of assuming that we are not protected at all, for we will never know what did not happen to us today.) Perhaps that can be blamed on our refusal to find His light, or perhaps it is a result of our walking our own path. My experience often leads me to the conclusion that life has many pitfalls and traps and other kinds of bad that just happen to us, even when we are doing our best to follow Him.

Another way "fear not" can trick us is when we assume a posture of personal invincibility. We are going to be strong. We forget the "for the Lord your God will be with you" part.

We want to face life on our own, being strong, counting on victory. We think ourselves able to fashion eagle wings, mounting up on our own creations, our own strength, our own ideas. Like Icarus, we are bound to discover that our creations, good as they may appear, are bound to melt when we pass, as we inevitably will, too close to the sun. We fall, wondering where the strength went and why Jesus is silent.

And David spoke the words of this song to the Lord in the day that the Lord delivered him from the hand of all his enemies and from the hand of Saul. And he said, "The Lord is my rock and my fortress and my deliverer; my God, my rock, in whom I take refuge; my shield and the horn of my salvation, my stronghold and my refuge; my savior, Thou dost save me from violence. I call upon the Lord, who is worthy to be praised; and I am saved from my enemies." (2 Samuel 22:1-4, NAS)

The Lord is my light and my salvation;
Whom shall I fear?
The Lord is the defense of my life;
Whom shall I dread?
When evildoers came upon me to devour my flesh,
My adversaries and my enemies, they stumbled and fell.
Though a host encamp against me,
My heart will not fear;
Though war arise against me,
In spite of this I shall be confident. (Psalm 27:1-4, NAS)

Do you ever read the words of David and wonder in what world he lived?

As I write this, war continues in the Middle East over issues that we do not fully understand. What we do understand is that the opposing sides have hated each other for a thousand years. What we do understand is that we are embroiled in this war, and that the ferocity of the battle grows by the hour. It grows ever closer to our sons and daughters.

Sickness crowds in at our door. Whether it is Alzheimer's, with its insidious, incurable grasp on memory and dignity, or lupus with inexplicable and debilitating flare-ups, or cancer that overshadows what was only yesterday a clean bill of health, disease seems inevitable. I am not writing at random. I am writing of my church, my friends, my family.

We see the news report devastating weather patterns and despicable crimes and seemingly unsolvable economic spirals, and fear seems unavoidable.

Be clear. God does not prevent the mountains from shaking in the very heart of the sea. God makes us no promises that we will not get sick or that our son will not get drafted or that the foaming waters will not roar over our heads. He makes no promises of ease and leisure.

God does not promise that life will be free of turmoil and strife. We are all quite certain that there have been, are now, and will continue to be times of trouble.

Why, then, does David have the nerve to say that he will not fear? Is it because we are immune from the storms of life? No. Is it because the koinonia of believers just makes it all OK? No, not that either.

Well, then, it must be that following God steels our nerve and sets our mind so that we travel on our own personal mountains of transfiguration where the glory of God keeps any real pain away from us. Tell that to the dutiful Christian who has just seen her child die. Tell that to Debbie, whose faithfulness to my church was cut short by her own battle with lupus for years, and to whose tribulations were added a husband awaiting a heart transplant and a new diagnosis of multiple sclerosis, not only for herself, but for her daughter.

I think that the answer lies in the midst of His people, where He builds community unknown anywhere else. He is our God. We do not travel these weary roads alone. Instead, we are His song carried by Him to the ears of the multitudes. We are as stones during the rain, cleansed by the power that surrounds us. We operate not on our own but rather as His hands, for He is with us, directing and embracing us.

Our celebration of God does not come because we live in a problem-free world. We do not celebrate His benevolence because He has calmed all of our storms and eliminated any times of trouble – He does no such thing. What we celebrate is His presence. We do not fear because He is a very present help in times of trouble. Presence is promised as the mechanism for His unfailing care.

When Jesus walked on the water to His disciples, He did not calm their storm before saying "It is I, be not afraid." He told Jacob to go into Egypt without fear, "for I will be with you." Joshua was taught to "be strong and courageous, for the Lord is with you." That He is our guide is enough.

The Psalmist does not issue a challenge for us heroically to cry out for the seas to rage while we shake our fist. Rest assured, the waters will roar and foam whether we ask for them to or not. Rather, David's voice brings a peaceful word to us to be still and know that God is God. He is present, especially in our times of trouble. Especially when the mountains of our lives are shaken to their core, we will not fear.

Be careful with texts like this one. Yes, God is our shield, but from what? He did not shield thousands of people from Katrina's fury. He did not shield those workers in the World Trade Center from maniacs in airplanes. He did not shield Asian Christians from the Tsunami or innocent children in Oklahoma City from Timothy McVeigh. He does not shield all Christians from having critically ill children. He does not shield all of our families from divorce. And yet, the scripture says: "The Lord is my rock…."

I believe that scripture and faith teach us perspective. We have already noted that Noah was not shielded from the flood and that Shadrach and his friends were not saved from entering the fiery furnace. Jesus Himself was not spared the cross. Paul faced shipwreck, John coped with exile, Elijah met loneliness, Joseph was sold into slavery and then falsely accused of rape. Daniel found himself among lions, and Mary lost her son. Beethoven was deaf. Martin Luther was declared a heretic. Cancer strikes saints every day. For Stephen, for Abel, for martyrs through the ages, there was no shield from death itself.

Still, the scripture is not vain. Noah walked out of the ark, Shadrach out of the furnace, and Jesus out of the grave. Beethoven gave us "Ode to Joy," and Stephen prayed, "Lord, do not hold this sin against them."

For our hope, our shield, our shelter is not so mundane as to protect us from the rain or the disease or the weapons of war. Oh yes, sometimes God does protect us from those things, and I certainly believe we should pray for that kind of protection. But that is not what we rely on and sing about.

What we sing about is God's amazing grace. The perspective of scripture looks far beyond this world, this time, this limited arena called earth where we play out our drama for a few short years. The Book of Job teaches that our storms and our afflictions are but a part of a supernatural "tour de force," and the gospel teaches us that for those who accept His grace, there is life in spite of death. The promise of life is ours forever – storm or no storm, cancer or no cancer, bankruptcy or plenty. A place in His glory with our Christ is prepared for us.

This is not a cop out. We do not look helplessly at war or natural disaster, realize we have nothing tangible to offer, and thus default to singing about the sweet bye and bye. Oh no. This is a recognition that we live in a world fraught with dangers, toils, and snares. And hurricanes. And terrorists. And deadly disease. "We are hard pressed on every side, but not crushed; perplexed, but not in despair; persecuted, but not abandoned; struck down, but not destroyed" (2 Corinthians 4:8-9 NIV). The only honest way to read that scripture is to acknowledge that we will be hard pressed, perplexed, persecuted, and struck down. In this world, devastation will come. Still, we sing.

Why? Because our hope alone is His amazing grace.

I cannot find a promise in scripture that says we will not pass through the valley of the shadow of death. What I find is just the opposite. That is where the promise of the prophet comes back to me. I am not protected from that shadow, but lo, though I most assuredly do walk through the valley of the shadow of death, He is with me. His rod and His staff comfort me. I am made strong. Despite the snares, shadows, and the darts hurled, I am protected wherever I go. Even when I am weak, He is strong.

So we come to the Lord facing life's fires and floods. The abuse, disease, and unfairness still confront us. We come to the Lord knowing that fear may follow us. Yet that Christian wife knows that she will not be swept over. Our brother knows that AIDS may defeat his body, but his soul cannot be consumed. We come to the Lord, and in remembrance of what He has done for us, we know that, ultimately, we are not afraid.

"Take courage. It is I. Don't be afraid."

When You Pray for God to Use You, Do You Really Want Your Prayer Answered?

Did you know that "prayer" is a legal term? That is right – whenever I file a motion or a complaint or a petition, I end it with a prayer. I "pray" that the court will do what I have asked, whether it be to grant my motion or dismiss the case filed against my client or give my client what he or she wants.

The story is told of the young lawyer who was arguing his first motion in court and doing a really bad job of it. As he struggled through the argument, the judge turned to the end of the lawyer's written motion to see that he had ended it improperly. The judge interrupted the lawyer by saying, "Son, you don't have a prayer." The lawyer quickly responded, "I know, your honor, but I am doing the best that I can!"

We should always end our legal papers with a prayer. Isn't that interesting? We lawyers do not even think about it; we just do it.

In our lives, we often throw a prayer into the mix out of habit, without really thinking about what we are doing. We pray because we have to, or because we are supposed to, or because we have nothing better to do; but, whatever the reason for the prayer, we do not wait for the answer. Sometimes, we do not see the answer to our prayers. More often, I think, we do not really want our prayers answered.

That statement seems oxymoronic, or maybe just moronic. Of course we want our prayers answered! Why else do we pray?

I think that our focus is off. I think that our aim is on ourselves, not on God and His will. Of course we are good at saying that our focus is on God, that our hope is built on nothing less than Jesus' blood and righteousness, that He is our soul's desire. I think we mean it, but I think that we often have no clue how to do it. What ends up being true is that we want our focus to be God, but we cannot get ourselves out of the way.

Self-focus is a subtle, discreet enemy. I am not suggesting that we set out to please ourselves. To the contrary, we set out to follow God. The problem is that somewhere along the way, we get satisfied with what we have offered

God. We become overwhelmed by our own promised willingness to sacrifice and forget to follow through and actually sacrifice.

This self-focus is seen both in an "I" sense and in a "we" sense. Call it "philanthropy" or "anthropomorphism" or "humanitarianism," but it manifests itself when we point at our brothers and sisters and praise them for their stated readiness to go to "deepest, darkest Africa" as veterinary missionaries if that is where God leads. The fact is that God is calling very few of us to Zimbabwe to become sheep doctors, so that is a pretty safe declaration for us to make. Please understand, I am not suggesting that we should not state a willingness to follow God wherever he leads. I am suggesting that praising our willingness to go is people-centered; going is God-centered.

We read with great reverence the story of Isaiah's call in the sixth chapter of his book.

> *In the year of King Uzziah's death, I saw the Lord sitting on a throne, lofty and exalted, with the train of His robe filling the temple. Seraphim stood above Him, each having six wings; with two he covered his face, and with two he covered his feet, and with two he flew. And one called out to another and said,*
>
> *"Holy, Holy, Holy, is the Lord of hosts, The whole earth is full of His glory."*
>
> *And the foundations of the thresholds trembled at the voice of him who called out, while the temple was filling with smoke. Then I said,*
>
> *"Woe is me, for I am ruined! Because I am a man of unclean lips, And I live among a people of unclean lips; For my eyes have seen the King, the Lord of hosts."*
>
> *Then one of the seraphim flew to me, with a burning coal in his hand which he had taken from the altar with tongs. And he touched my mouth with it and said, "Behold, this has touched your lips; and your iniquity is taken away, and your sin is forgiven." Then I heard the voice of the Lord, saying, "Whom shall I send, and who will go for Us?" Then I said, "Here am I. Send me!"* (Isaiah 6:1-8, NAS)

What a great passage of commitment! This story of the calling of the prophet Isaiah mirrors the words of other great prophets of God. When God called to Abraham to test him, Abraham's response was "Here I am." At the burning bush, Moses said to the Lord "Here I am." When God called the sleeping Samuel, the child's response was "Here I am."

My friend Cathy Self placed an image in my head that makes so very much sense. Think back to when you were in the second grade. School was still fun and you were anxious to please. Authority made sense. When your teacher said she needed a helper, that she had a job to be done, you joined the class in raising your hand as high as a seven-year-old can, straining for attention, calling out, "Here I am. Pick me. Am I the one?" You did not know what the task was. You did not care. All you knew was that your teacher needed help, and you wanted to help. In fact, you begged to be the one chosen. "Here I am – PICK ME!!!"

As His children, we hear Him calling to us. We say that His authority makes sense to us. We sometimes announce that we are committed to Him, and we know that He has a job to be done. Actually, we know that He has many jobs to be done. We do not always perceive which job He has for us. We may not see where He is leading us, and sometimes we may not even feel His leadership at all, but we know that His light must be borne and His word must be spoken.

We cannot pray this prayer if we think that "Here I am, Lord" is our response to God. We should, instead, pray "Here I am, Lord" and anticipate with faith God's response to us.

The trouble is that we stop reading at verse 8, and we are all moved at Isaiah's solemn declaration of "Here I am Lord, send me." We get a romantic view of crusades and harp playing and becoming a great prophet. We do not read the rest of the story. It is not even a new paragraph; it is simply the obvious continuation of the account:

> *Then I heard the voice of the Lord, saying, "Whom shall I send, and who will go for Us?" Then I said, "Here am I. Send me!" And He said, "Go, and tell this people: 'Keep on listening, but do not perceive; keep on looking, but do not understand.' Render the hearts of this people insensitive, their ears dull, and their eyes dim, lest they see with their eyes, hear with their ears, understand with their hearts, and return and be healed." Then I said, "Lord, how long?" And He answered, "Until cities are devastated and without inhabitant, houses are without people, and the land is utterly desolate. "The Lord has removed men far away, and the forsaken places are many in the midst of the land." (Isaiah 6:8-11, NAS)*

You see, when Isaiah said "Here I am Lord," God said, "Go." God sent him to preach to people who would not understand and who would be openly hostile to his message and who would turn from God until at last they were taken away into exiled captivity by a foreign power. That is not nearly so romantic. Focusing on God means not so much praising ourselves and our contemporaries for saying, "Here I am," as it means obeying God when he says, "Go." Not nearly as romantic, but much more important.

While committing to incredible foreign projects if it is God's will can be a heady experience that brings us the admiration of good Christian cohorts, it is more sobering to tell God "Here I am, Lord" when the cause is around the corner and well within our means. Excuses about our own abilities and fears of possible negative responses blind us to the strength of our God, the Lord of sea and sky who made the stars and the snow and the rain. We forget that God takes care of the poor and lame, satisfies His people with the finest of the wheat, and has given His very life for us. He has promised to brighten the darkest soul and break the stone coldness of the most sinful heart. Our memories of those promises pale as we hesitate to obey. The faith we are so eager to display when the chances of His actually calling on us are slim (and I assure you that the chances of my being called anywhere as a veterinarian are slim) too often evaporates when He truly answers our prayer of commitment and calls for our help.

When Jesus walked on the water toward his disciples, what do you remember about Peter? Too often, we remember his telling Jesus: "Lord, if it is really you, then let me walk to you on the water." What I remember is that Jesus, without a second's hesitation, answered, "Come." As the saying goes, be careful what you pray for; you will probably get it.

Peter's prayer was answered immediately, affirmatively, and clearly. What I remember is not that Peter boasted that he had the faith to walk on the water. What I remember is that Peter got out of the boat and walked on the water.

I think that, too often, our focus is on ourselves, not on our Creator… on our prayers, not on His answers to those prayers. In fact, I am not really sure that we want our prayers answered. We want to say that we are ready to walk on the water and we want people to hear our willingness to walk on water, but we don't want to get out of the boat. We dutifully put a "prayer" at the end of the motion we have filed with the court, but we do not really think about why we must "pray" and what happens if the judge interrupts to tell us that we do not have a prayer.

"Lord, if it is really you, then let me come to you on the sea." "OK, come on."

"Whom shall I send, and who will go for us?" "Here am I Lord, send me." "OK, Go."

May we mean what we pray, may we listen for the answer, and may we count on Him to provide as we do what He asks.

Open My Eyes, Lord

I beseech you therefore, brethren, by the mercies of God, that ye present your bodies a living sacrifice, holy, acceptable unto God, which is your reasonable service. (Romans 12:1, KJV)

This is one of those verses that we learned in Sunday School when we were children, when the King James was still used for memory verses. Maybe you understood that verse then, but to my fifth grade mind, it made little sense.

Now that I am an adult, the idea of complete submission – of surrendering all and saying "wherever He leads, I'll go" – often still does not register. Intellectually, it makes sense to say because God's mercy is so amazing, because it is so wide, because He is so faithful in providing us with a fount of new blessings every morning, therefore we owe everything to Him and should respond to Him by submitting, sacrificing ourselves to His every loving command.

Realistically I do not live according to the logical dictates that my Bible study and my spiritual knowledge provide. Experientially, I tend to rely on the mercy of God, knowing that He is loving and forgiving, without responding to it with the obedience He requires and the meekness He modeled for us.

When your logical understanding of the call of Christ and your reasonable response to Him crash against the reality of your daily life and all the claims placed upon you by the world, the result is often something other than a presentation of yourself as a sacrifice to God. The result of that meeting is often simply a crash.

To me, one of the most amazing things about God is that He enables His children, at least those humble enough to ask, to follow His call. The stunning thing about prayer is not always the miraculous healing or the rescue from the pit. Instead, the power of prayer is often found in our recognition that we cannot see, that our steps are out of whack, and that we are not sure how to serve or follow.

Surrender does not mean that we figure out a neat thing to do for God today. Instead, a living sacrifice is waiting on the Lord, looking around to see what He is doing, and then joining when He invites us. Submission does not mean that we stop, look, and listen. Instead, we pray for our Creator to open our eyes and ears. I think that is what it means to see with "spirit eyes" and to hear with "spirit ears."

Humility lies in recognizing that our desires, when left to our own devices, are reflections of our sinful nature. Scripture's promise that God gives to those who trust in Him the desires of their heart means exactly what it says. When we submit to Him, He replaces our selfish and short-sighted wishes and wants with a heart that seeks after Him. A heart that wants what He wants. He inclines our heart toward Himself and literally gives us new desires, which He in turn willingly satisfies.

I pray to get effect, not just to change myself (the famous and oft-quoted words of Anthony Hopkins, playing C.S. Lewis in "Shadowlands", notwithstanding), for I believe that God truly responds to all of our prayers and grants many of them. But, during the crash of what I know with what I want, I have to pray so that I can be changed. God is always the same God, but I must once again let Him be to me a God whom I love, adore, worship, follow, and serve. I must change before I am ready to look to God.

There is a famous prayer that goes like this:

"Open Thou mine eyes, that I may see.
Incline my heart, that I may desire.
Order my steps, that I may walk in the way of Thy commandments.
O Lord my God, be Thou to me a God, and beside Thee, let there be none other.
Vouchsafe to me to worship Thee and serve Thee in truth of spirit, in reverence of body, in blessing of lips, in public and private."

I take great comfort in knowing that the author of this prayer, Sir Lancelot Andrews, was an extraordinary Christian and churchman. He was, among other things, Bishop of Chichester and Ely, Dean of Westminster, and participant in the coronation of King James I. Because he was a member of the Hampton Court Conference, Andrews' name appears in the introduction to the King James Bible as being one of the primary influences in the creation of that great English translation for the people. Society cohort of Sir Walter Raleigh and affectionate supporter of a young writer named John Calvin, Bishop Andrews is remembered to this day in the Anglican Church as the "great light of the Christian world."

Why the history lesson? Because the words of his prayer, if we take them halfway seriously, bring us into a stark recognition of our weakness, our failure, our gross inadequacy.

It is only the blind who need to pray for their eyes to be opened. Only if our steps are out of order do we need help to walk in His ways. To "vouchsafe" is to grant graciously something to someone who does not deserve it, so it is only the one who is otherwise unwilling or unable to worship and serve who prays this prayer, one who is concerned about the truthfulness of his spirit, one who may be ashamed of what she has done with her body, one whose words betray a tendency to say things that are far from blessing.

It is a comfort to me that someone like Sir Lancelot, great Anglican preacher, found in himself the need to pray this prayer. It is like reading the Apostle Paul when he writes: "I do not understand what I do. For what I want to do I do not do, but what I hate I do…. As it is, it is no longer I myself who do it, but it is sin living in me. I know that nothing good lives in me, that is, in my sinful nature. For I have the desire to do what is good, but I cannot carry it out. For what I do is not the good I want to do; no, the evil I do not want to do—this I keep on doing." (Romans 7:15-19, NIV) If the Bishop of Chichester and the missionary apostle himself fought this battle, then maybe I am not such an outcast. Maybe I am not beyond forgiveness. If they were so weak and failed so often, maybe there is hope for me to be of some use to God.

How wonderful that God answers our prayers! How blessed we are that He answers this prayer, and that He changes us. He will open our eyes, and He will order our steps to walk in the ways of His commandments. After all, in light of the amazing mercy He has shown to us, that is our reasonable service.

Are you like me? Do you have your own translation of Sir Lancelot's prayer? "O God, forgive me and help me, for I am helpless on my own. I am blind – open my eyes. I am prone to wander – order my steps. My desires are sinful – incline my heart. I find myself seeking and finding other gods that push you out of the way. Give me the grace to acknowledge you in worship and in action, despite my lies, my lusts, my curses. I cannot control myself. Only you can open eyes, supervise steps, push away all others. Please do. For I am needy."

Amen.

The Poetry and Music of Prayer

Then you will call upon Me and come and pray to Me, and I will listen to you. And you will seek Me and find Me, when you search for Me with all your heart. (Jeremiah 29:12-13, NAS)

Legal writing is one of those required first-year classes in law school that often is met with yawns and grudging attendance. It is not nearly as exciting as the "new" ideas like torts and procedure, and students tend to take it for granted. It is often not until we get into the actual practice of law that we appreciate our law school's requirement that we learn the rhetoric of attorneys and the structure of how lawyers write. The law requires a language all its own to get across to a specialized audience some unique and particular ideas.

Prayer is not much different. While anyone can pray using whatever words he or she knows, we discover that prayer often is significantly aided by a language of its own to get across some specific and critical ideas to a very special audience. An audience of One.

"Poetry is a subconscious conversation; it is as much the work of those who understand it as those who make it."

These words of poet Sonia Sanchez speak volumes about our attempts at prayer. The work of the Psalmist or the hymn writer or the lyricist is to put down on paper not just words, but symbolic attempts to characterize God. When we pray, we somehow must capture that characterization into our own brand of poetry and music. Our work as speaker is matched with the work of God as He relates to us and speaks to us, even as we speak. Such prayer begins to allow these words to become more than just words.

Jesus cannot be captured in mere human words, even words as graceful and flowing and meaningful as the greatest hymn or the most majestic Psalm. To describe Christ as "the joy of loving hearts" is undoubtedly true. He is unquestionably "the fount of life" and "the light of men." Thankfully, He saves those who call on Him.

But these are still words, and they are still human, and they still want.

I would paraphrase the words of Sanchez to note that prayer is, or should be, indeed must be, a conscious conversation. We must work just as hard to understand as to speak. If our prayers consist of nothing more than our repeated thanks for His gracious smile, if our prayer is simply a plea for Christ to stay with us, then we miss much of the point, much as mere words miss their aim of describing our Lord.

Is there someone you love to hear pray? When I ask myself that question, the person who immediately springs to mind is Jeff Simmons, the former Minister to Students at my church who is now a pastor in Franklin, Tennessee. When Jeff prays - before the entire congregation from the pulpit, during a baptismal service from the small pool behind the choir loft, or in a private setting with just the two of us over lunch - there is no question that Jeff is having conversation with his closest friend. His love for God and his real desire to please God are matched by an honest effort to communicate, to tell God what is on his mind and to seek what is on God's mind. The words do not rhyme, but Jeff's discussions with God ring with the music of poetry.

Christ will not be put in any manmade box. He deserves more than we can muster. He demands simply all that we are. He seeks the beauty of poetry and the relationship of conversation.

Some Christians look at prayer as an attitude. We walk in His steps, as best we can, and we do His will, as best we can, and that keeps us close to Him. That relationship is, for some, prayer.

Some look at prayer as a ritual. Not a ritual in a bad way, like having to kiss Aunt Gertrude or fight the crowds on the morning after Thanksgiving; instead, a treasured tradition that comes every meal, every night before sleep, every Sunday.

Some look at prayer as a worship device. It is an intentional articulation of the greatness of God. Praise and adoration are part and parcel with prayer. It is a moment of recognition of God, who is greater than we and who is looking over us.

Some look at prayer as a rescue system. There are no atheists in foxholes, and there are few Christians who do not turn to prayer in times of deepest despair, illness, loss, confusion, and disappointment.

Some look at prayer as a spiritual marker. Spending time in prayer, honestly analyzing our actions and attitudes, and gauging what kind of a response we "feel" or "hear" are ways of letting some of us know if we are where we need to be.

Some look at prayer as a way to get things done. Ask and it shall be given; seek and you shall find. We believe the promises and we see things that we think should be changed; so we ask God, within the bounds of His will, to change them.

Some look at prayer as a check on our own sinfulness. We have found through experience that we cannot honestly be in the presence of God without being changed. What we had intended or wanted is altered by our prayerful encounter with the divine. In these cases, prayer is not to find an answer so much as it is to change us as we experience the one true God.

Some look at prayer as a welcome Christian duty, an opportunity to intercede for those in need.

Some look at prayer as a joy, an opportunity to revel in God.

Some look at prayer as rest, as a place to go where we know what we will find, where we know we are accepted and loved, and where burdens can be left.

Jesus looked at prayer as a necessity. He modeled it at Lazarus' tomb, in Gethsemane, in the River Jordan, at the Last Supper, on the mountainside with five thousand hungry listeners, on the cross.

I think prayer is all these things. I think we have little real understanding of everything that prayer can be, but I think we learn a little more each time we pray.

Then what? Then we trust Christ. He specializes in subconscious conversation. We trust Him to chase the dark night of sin away. He trusts us to share the poetry.

Every once in a while, I have discovered, you can learn a real spiritual truth from your pastor. It was my pastor Frank Lewis (no relation to C.S. as far as I know) who interpreted a familiar verse from Romans 8 in a way that had escaped me.

In the same way, the Spirit helps us in our weakness. We do not know what we ought to pray for, but the Spirit himself intercedes for us with groans that words cannot express. (Romans 8:26, NIV)

I could not rise above an issue of great consequence to my spiritual life, and I had no idea what God's will was for the situation, so I had no idea how to pray within God's will. Frank's response was simple. He told me, "Just pray. The Spirit will get it right."

How simple, yet how profound. I had interpreted this verse to mean that if I did not know the precise three-dollar-word to get God's attention, the Holy Spirit would pray in Aramaic for me to solve the problem. Once again, I was guilty of boxing God in to my limited understanding. It is not just when we don't know the language. It is when we cannot begin to know what we want or how even to approach a problem that the Spirit helps us in our weakness. We do not know even for what to pray, but we have the faith to turn to the Father and attempt to pray.

We are in the Psalmist's pit. We want to rise.

I think that the poetry of prayer, when prayed by the Spirit, is musical. I think that when our feeble attempts at prayer are no more than groans, the Spirit in us sings, and the Spirit becomes our helper. He takes our often pitiful attempts and turns them into real poetry, real music. I think God the Father longs to hear the music of God the Spirit, just as He longed for the angels' song on the hills outside Bethlehem or the creation song of the morning stars singing together for joy.

Together, even as a church, we can be in the bog. We need to rise. We do not know how to approach the throne, but we know that we can, and we must approach the throne of grace with confidence. We do not know how to rise, how to lift our dreary souls from the mire, but He lifts us up as His Spirit takes us where our words alone cannot go on wings of song and prayer.

On a German opera house, these words appear: "Bach gave us God's word. Mozart gave us God's laughter. Beethoven gave us God's fire. God gave us music, that we might pray without words."

We must rise. Sing. Let your music lift your soul's prayer beyond where your words can take it. Let the notes give wing to that prayer. With the faith of a child, or of a German builder, know that the Spirit is taking you where you must go, lifting you out of the miry bog and stretching to heaven itself. You have the poetry within you. The song of prayer is waiting only for you and the Holy Spirit to join in sacred duet.

It is an exercise in faith.

Rise. Rise. Rise.

A New Day of Praise

I will praise you, O LORD, with all my heart; I will tell of all your wonders. I will be glad and rejoice in you; I will sing praise to your name, O Most High. (Psalm 9:1-2, NIV)

As you read the Psalms and see David and the other writers finding still more new, wonderful words of praise, it becomes formulaic to repeat some of the words in a clichéd catechism of praise. It can be hard to come up with something new to say or a new way to praise God, and that is the point that I think needs to be made. Praise does not always come easy – not because we do not want to praise, and not because we are sunk so deep in sin that we cannot praise – but simply because we feel that we've "been there, done that" so much that we cannot generate anything original and sincere.

That is when God surprises us. When the Sauls of our world turn out to be jealous old men who have turned from the Lord to their own selfishness, we expect God to replace them with the best and the brightest and the most famous and the best educated. God instead sends an old prophet to anoint a young shepherd boy who turns out to be David – King, Psalmist, father of the temple-builder, slayer of Goliath, and forefather of the house and lineage of Jesus Christ.

When we have finished singing Hosanna to His blessed name and praising Him for His mighty works, He reveals His mightiest work to us, Jesus himself, and we discover that God's love is boundless. Not just great, not even greater than the love from anyone else - boundless.

When we have begun to mature as Christians and the story of Christ's death for our sins becomes a comfortable Sunday School memory that does not bring us much meaning today, we inevitably fall. Then God surprises us, not with the expected rebuke and deserved reprisal, but with His love and forgiveness that turns our failures inside out. We see Jesus' face anew, and God's incredible grace is shining from it.

I got surprised one weekend a few years ago after we had met our new friend Evan, the day after his birth. About a block from the hospital, in a driving rainstorm, stood a thin woman in obvious distress. She was crying her eyes out and waiving for anyone to stop. We picked her up in the minivan. As we began driving, she was too hysterical to make any sense of her situation, but she found from somewhere the impetus for a repeated verbal prayer of "Thank you, Jesus."

Eventually, we learned that her house had been destroyed by fire and the agency to which she had walked before the cloudburst had no money to help her. She was desperate, but she was also faithful. As we drove to the ATM so we could give her a little help, she continued to pray out loud. I heard her say, "Lord, you told me that if I had faith the size of a mustard seed you would move the mountain, and now I see you doing it. Oh Lord, thank you!" Her name was Tonya.

I guess I was not expecting the small, hysterical woman in the rain to be a woman of exceptionally articulate faith. It was surprising to find a beacon of hope in her almost emaciated body. God surprised me when I took a tiny step of stopping a van for a woman in a rainstorm by granting a quick harvest for me and providing a necessary emergency provision for her. Maybe Tonya was surprised that Gena and I stopped and helped, but there is no way she was as surprised as I was by her amazing faith in soul-trying circumstances. She did not know us, and we did not know her, but the Holy Spirit recognizes Himself when Christians come into contact with one another. That should not be a surprise, but it almost always is.

Before the surprise, we have trouble coming up with why we are singing to the Lord. But, when God startles us into seeing that His grace is shining on us again, just as it always has been, we wish we had a thousand tongues to sing our Redeemer's praise.

What is the first scripture you remember memorizing as a child? Is it John 3:16? The Twenty-Third Psalm? "Jesus wept?"

For me, it is Psalm 100. It was in children's choir in the first grade. Oh, I suppose I could say the Lord's Prayer before that, but I was not cognizant that that was "scripture." Learning Psalm 100 on Wednesday nights was an exercise that for some reason has stuck in my head.

I have always been struck by the concept in that psalm of joyful noise. The focus is on the manner of praise, the exuberance, and the sheer pleasure that should surround our worship offerings to God. The focus is not on the style of worship, the complication of the chord structure or the eight-part voicing, or even the content of what we say. We are to serve the Lord with gladness. We are to enter His courts with praise, regardless of our circumstances. We must give thanks to Him and praise His holy name even when we are not thankful, when we are not glad, when we are not jubilant.

You see, the psalm does not speak to our emotion. It speaks in spite of our emotion. We make a joyful noise simply because we know that the Lord is God. It is He that has made us, and not we ourselves. We are His people and the sheep of His pasture.

Hear me well – God does care about our content and excellence. There are those who use "a joyful noise" as an excuse to offer poor worship, just so long as it is loud. That is not the point. The point is that we are first to be jubilant. We are first to praise, to thank, to sing.

To everything, there is a season. There is a time for confession, for mourning, for honest expressions of gloom as we humble ourselves before the Lord. But we come first with joy, praise, and thanksgiving. It is why the Model Prayer begins, before our trespasses and our need for daily bread, with awestruck worship – "Hallowed be Thy name."

Parenting three babies added a new perspective to me on this point. I rejoiced to hear the first joyful noises from my babies when they saw me peering through the bars of the crib or playing peek-a-boo across a dinner table. That did not mean that I wanted them to stay in the goo-goo stage forever. Now I take great pleasure in hearing their mature, more complicated, more substantive words of love to me. But when they could do nothing else, they could still make a joyful noise, and as their father, I was pleased. I would do whatever I could, make whatever face, or sing whatever silly ditty to get them to do it again.

I think that is what God does. He longs to hear our joyful praise, and when He hears it, He says to us, "That's great. Do it again!"

Let's do it again.

When yesterday's praise does not come easy on this new day, it is the time to prepare to sing to the Lord a joyful song, to quote that favorite psalm, to repeat that almost-hackneyed prayer – for the surprise of God is just around the corner.

And for each of us, God has our own moment, our own unique glimpse into God's glory. What is it for you? I am talking about that rarest of gifts that God has for His children on only those occasions when He decides to open His treasure chest.

It is the gift, often no more than a nanosecond, which induces that purest form of praise, the alleluia. Some call it an "aha" moment. Some describe it as a brief glimpse of heaven. Some don't call it anything, for they are moved to a place beyond words.

It does not happen often. I am not talking about praise that we offer as a part of a planned worship experience, or as a part of adoration beginning our prayer time, or even in response to an answered prayer. Those are all legitimate, valuable, and typical.

But there is something else that constitutes a heart of passion, a fervor. The purest form of reverence is but rarely experienced by any of us. It is the extraordinary, uncommon moment when our spirit truly experiences His Spirit clearly. Yes, one day that will be common, for we shall see Him as He is; for now, except when the gift is given, we see though a glass darkly.

So when is it for you? Is it sitting in a certain sanctuary, cathedral, or chapel? Is it hearing a choir sing the Hallelujah Chorus or a moving spiritual? Is it walking in the Alps just as the clouds break, revealing the Matterhorn suddenly before you in its splendor? Is it witnessing the birth of your child? Is it holding the hand of a Christian as his soul passes into eternity with His father? Is it singing "How Great Thou Art" or "Joy to the World?"

For Moses, it was taking off his shoes and hearing a disembodied voice from a burning bush that was not consumed. For Nebuchadnezzer, it was watching three boys walk out of an execution chamber. For Ezekiel, it was watching skeletons put on some skin and begin to dance. For Mary, it was a visit from an angel with a challenge and a promise. For Peter, after a denial, it was finding the Lord standing unexpectedly, waiting for him on a beach. For Thomas, it was the moment His risen Lord held out a bloody hand and invited him to touch the wounds.

For Jean Valjean, it was every time he looked at the bishop's candlesticks. For Eric Liddle, it was running fast and feeling God's pleasure. For the folk singer, it is touching a leaf. For the waiting father, it was seeing the prodigal on the road home. For St. Francis of Assisi, it was experiencing the golden beam of the rising sun, the softer gleam of the silver moon, the voices of the evening stars.

I don't think it is the same for any of us. What is critical is that we look for it, that we do not miss it. For it is not an everyday occurrence. Yes, His mercies are new every morning, our prayers always have His attention, He walks with us daily. I join you in sincerest gratitude for all of that. But beyond the everyday, He has a special gift for His children, a gift that He dispenses carefully and infrequently, a peek into His presence, a foretaste of glory divine.

Don't stop with the surprise, the enjoyment of the newness of the experience. Don't forget the praise. Do not fail to move from "aha" to "alleluia."

For the Lord is good. His mercy is everlasting. And His truth endures to all generations.

That's great!

Do it again, children!

What Is Your Treasure?

I suppose it is too easy a target to point at most of my attorney colleagues (not myself, of course!) as money-grubbing misers who would not be seen in public without driving the right car and wearing the right wristwatch and drinking the right drink; so I won't make that point. I will take the opportunity to point out that most of what we civil lawyers do is fight over money, property, stuff. Even when the issue is important and personal, like personal injuries or medical malpractice or divorce, the way that "justice" is done is to award or deny the award of money. It is truly what makes the wheels of the law turn.

Do not store up for yourselves treasures on earth, where moth and rust destroy, and where thieves break in and steal. But store up for yourselves treasures in heaven, where moth and rust do not destroy, and where thieves do not break in and steal. For where your treasure is, there your heart will be also. (Matthew 6:19-21, NIV)

These words are familiar, maybe too familiar. Maybe so familiar that we lose the words of Christ in the words of the stereotypical televangelist: "Do not keep your treasures here on earth, O selfish one. You better give lots of money to this min'stry – we call that storing up treasure in heaven. 'Cause if you don't do it, your heart can't go to heaven."

Of course, our natural reaction is to flinch, mutter under our breath, toss a few mites into the plate, and hope that the bothersome money grubbers will go away, at least until next year.

I don't think this portion of the Sermon on the Mount is in any way intended to make us feel uncomfortable or guilty or even particularly bothered. I think that Jesus is, as usual, giving practical advice for those who bother to pay attention to Him. I am not even convinced He is talking about money, at least not completely or primarily.

No, the focus of these words is not on commanding us to sacrifice but rather on pointing out that things on earth do not last. Moths and rust are facts of life here. Just as we benefit from the simple gifts of light and water, we cannot get away from bugs that are drawn to the light or from chemical reactions. Ever since Eve ate the apple, the natural processes have not been the only things causing us to find ourselves losing things; we have to watch out for each other's thieving ways.

God provides His dear children not just with happy thoughts and warm fuzzy feelings but with security, in eternity where there are no moths or thieves and where even rust cannot tarnish us.

In that light, we give back to God. Our giving is not a grudging response to a guilt-laden pep talk. Generosity naturally grows out of what we have been given. Consider the birds of the air, for they do not sow, neither do they reap, but your heavenly Father feeds them. Consider the lilies of the field, for they do not toil, neither do they spin, yet Solomon in all his glory was not arrayed like one of these.

The point of this part of the Sermon on the Mount is that our earthly ways, ideas, and priorities are ultimately fruitless. That is true because our desires and thoughts are evil even when we can resist the temptations of murder or adultery, because we do not understand the value of meekness or purity of heart. It is true because we spend far too much time crying, "Lord, Lord" and far too little doing the will of our Father. It is true because we invest in things that we cannot keep – things that cannot help but be destroyed, or stolen, or both.

As Jim Elliot wrote in his journal weeks before his death, he is no fool who gives up what he cannot keep to gain what he cannot lose.

Money will always be the earthly way. I know no better way to compensate the victim of malpractice or to provide for the suddenly fatherless child. My point is not that Jesus is attacking money but instead to demonstrate that while money is important on earth, it is only on earth that stuff is of importance. The point of these words is that Jesus offers us security from our earthly thoughts, failures, and losses. What He offers us is treasure in heaven. We need not fend off moths or rust or thieves. All we need do is take the offer.

An Offer Worth Accepting

Perhaps the first basic of contract law is that a contract requires an offer and an acceptance.[1] That makes sense – to reach an agreement, two parties must have a starting place. The law calls that starting place the "offer." Perhaps I offer you a product, and you accept by paying a price. Or maybe I offer you a salary and you accept by taking a job. It could be that your company offers to pay for services and my company accepts by doing the work. A common contract is made when one person proposes marriage and the other accepts with a ring, a kiss, and an "I do."

God has an offer for us. I do not want to take the contract analogy too far, because we humans are by nature going to breach any contract we have with God. The courts where I practice would throw us out on our collective ear. The Father's mercy and forgiveness are certainly foreign to any court I know anything about.

Still, it is worth it to examine what God has offered us.

Peace I leave with you; my peace I give you. I do not give to you as the world gives. Do not let your hearts be troubled and do not be afraid. (John 14:27, NIV)

Therefore do not worry about tomorrow, for tomorrow will worry about itself. Each day has enough trouble of its own. (Matthew 6:34, NIV)

What are the promises of God? Do you find yourself trusting God for things that He has not offered? He clearly does not promise wealth or health or ease or happiness for every second of every day. In fact, an honest reading of scripture leads inescapably to the guarantee that life will bring suffering, attack, and crisis. That is a promise.

The gospel writers knew. The hymn writers get it. We too must understand and not shrink from the recognition that we must meet trials here, that every day involves a mix of pain and pleasure. Some of us reach a point of maturity where we can see, and even welcome, God's own hand – for whatever His purposes are – working to mingle toil with our rest.

What, then, are the promises of God?

---

[1] I have not forgotten my first year of law school. I know there are more elements of a contract. I am just focusing on offer and acceptance for the moment. In the next chapter, we will take a look at another requirement of contracts.

First, we are promised eternity. There is a promised land that we shall one day reach, and our toils and troubles will in fact be over.

We are promised strength in a measure sufficient for what our days have for us.

We are promised protection. Not that the arrows will never hit us, but that we can never be taken from the hand of Him whose very name is power.

We are promised presence. Every day, the Lord Himself is near me. Worry and fear come to some of us so naturally – and yet the gospel means that He is with us day by day, and with each passing moment. We are to take the days and moments from His hand.

We are promised consolation. We are assured not that we will avoid tribulation but rather that we will persevere despite the inevitable tribulation. This assurance comes through the scriptures and our faith and His pledge to take our yoke on Himself.

And, we are promised peace. Not as the world thinks of peace – an absence of hostility. War rages as I write these words, so the promises of God – if true, as I believe they are – do not mean that kind of "peace." Neither does this promise mean "peace" as the world gives peace – by going away and leaving us alone. For the world cries "peace, peace," and yet there is no peace. I do not believe any of us hopes that God's promise means that He will leave us to our own devices.

No, our peace is not something that is taken away from us. It is a positive that is added to us. Peace is our Father's gift, wisely bestowed on His beloved children. It is permanent, it is sufficient, it is divine, and it is necessary. We need it, and we have it, day by day, and with each passing moment.

"Peace I leave with you." That is an offer worth accepting.

Consideration – The Presence of God

Another basic rule of contracts is that there has to be consideration flowing both ways – there has to be an inducement for each party to enter into the contract. If we make a contract for me to sell you a horse, your consideration is that you get a horse; mine is that I get your money.

It is here that the contract analogy continues to fall down, because God's grace is not conditioned on our actions. We do not have to perform our part of the deal. His forgiveness means that consideration often flows only one way – His blessings come to us even when He gets nothing. We can and hopefully do commit amazing things to God, but he may not "get a horse." Still, He provides us an amazing thing – Himself. Jesus gave Himself on the cross for our sins, but that was not the end. Instead, it was the continuation of God's choice to walk with us – His flawed, selfish creatures – merely because He loves us. He still gives Himself as He is present with us.

God is our refuge and strength,
an ever-present help in trouble.
Therefore we will not fear, though the earth give way
and the mountains fall into the heart of the sea,
though its waters roar and foam
and the mountains quake with their surging. (Psalm 46:1-3, NIV)

Why do you worship God?

Is it because of His works? Do you thrill in telling others about the awesome acts of God?

Maybe it is because He has been, or is now, your refuge. You have experienced the most intense time of trouble imaginable, quaking mountains, and foaming waters. Your soul has found rest in God.

As human beings, we grow accustomed to God's creations and even His miracles, and we soon take them for granted. We do not always find ourselves among the roaring waves, and so we do not seek refuge.

Why then do we worship God?

The answer, I think, is because of His presence. He is a very present help. The first four words of the Bible make it very clear – "In the beginning, God."

My former college minister, David Johnson, tells the story of his two-year-old nephew who had spilled Pixy Stix candy over the floor of the family van. His parents found him in the van with a Dustbuster, moving the machine over the candy and saying, "Vroom, vroom." Of course, nothing was happening – the candy was not being picked up – because the appliance was not plugged into any power source.

We too can go through all the motions and make all the right noises, but if we are not connected to the power, our acts are worthless. If we are not connecting to the very presence of God, then all we really accomplish is to make everyone else wonder where we are and what we are doing.

In the wonderful movie "Chariots of Fire," Eric Liddle talks to those who have seen him win a race, telling them, "I can only point the way. I have no formula for winning the race. Everyone runs in her own way, or his own way. And where does the power come from, to see the race to its end? From within." God cannot be reduced to a miracle-working showman whose awesome acts demand our praise. He is not simply our refuge. He is very literally our strength.

The LORD himself goes before you and will be with you; he will never leave you nor forsake you. Do not be afraid; do not be discouraged. (Deuteronomy 31:8, NIV)

Worship can be found in the crescendo of the most majestic hymn, but it also includes time taken out from our routine to kneel before the Lord. Worship often is, simply put, time in the presence of the Lord.

Going through our lives and the ordinary, tedious challenges that we face daily, we don't always understand what God's perfect will demands of us. We are often more interested in racing through our obligations and trying our best to be home before the kids go to bed. The prophet, however, tells us that they who wait on the Lord will renew their strength.

There is great reward in that wait. We take the time to trust God more and remember His promise to be faithful. He reveals His wisdom that knows our deepest secrets, and He fills us with His peace, His comfort, and His grace.

The problem with our natural routine is that we forget the amazing, supernatural God, who invites us through His open door into His presence. We become filled with the battles that the world has to throw at us, instead of being grounded in the love of God. We lose our abilities – our ableness – because we forget that the strength that comes with the name of the Lord is found in His presence.

For I will turn their mourning into joy, and will comfort them, and give them joy for their sorrow. And I will fill the soul of the priests with abundance, and My people shall be satisfied with My goodness.... (Jeremiah 31:13-14, NAS)

Whom have I in heaven but you? And earth has nothing I desire besides you. My flesh and my heart may fail, but God is the strength of my heart and my portion forever. Those who are far from you will perish; you destroy all who are unfaithful to you. But as for me, it is good to be near God. (Psalm 73:25-28, NIV)

We can do nothing without God. We are weak and we fail. It is interesting that if you look up the words "strength" or "strengthen" in scripture, they inevitably are juxtaposed to our weakness. Isaiah explains that God strengthens weak hands and firms feeble knees. Paul tells us that God's grace is sufficient for us because His strength is made perfect in our weakness. The writer of Hebrews chronicles the heroes of the faith and says that out of their weakness, they were made strong.

Our strength comes not from our own trials and achievements. Instead, they that wait upon the Lord shall renew their strength. God has chosen the weak things of the world to confound the things that are mighty.

God is more than our power source. The nearness of God is good.

We look at ourselves, as the Psalmist looked at himself, and see nothing of real worth that we can bring to God. It astounds us that He nevertheless saw value in us when we were lost, blind, bitter, and without reason. He loved us enough to take hold of our hands and walk with us. Even to die for us.

My grandmother might have said that we are "no earthly good" to anyone. She would be right. Our good is not "earthly" at all; it is heavenly and spiritual. Our merit springs from a faith that the unseen strengthener of weak hands is among us now.

We thank God often for being present to comfort and to guide. Let us not forget to praise Him for being present for the sole reason that His presence is valuable. For me, it is good to be near God. Because He is here, there is something good about me.

I remember what mid-winter retreat meant to me. Every year, during the week between Christmas and New Year's, our youth group would travel for three days to Brandon Springs, at Land-Between-the-Lakes, Kentucky, for our retreat. Nearly one hundred teenagers, taking a break from school and family and routine, taking three days to focus on God and what He meant to each of us. We looked forward to a "high" that we knew awaited us, and He never failed to provide it.

Then we would come home, and the routine would begin again. For a fifteen year-old trying to live off of spiritual adrenaline, ordinary life could make Jesus seem far away.

Now, though, I have learned that spiritual adrenaline springing from a mountaintop experience is both short-lived and shallow. It is in the routine, non-special, repetitive times that the love of Christ is most real. Anybody can feel a rush from a big concert or feel "spiritual" after a retreat, but those who are able to comprehend how high and how wide and how deep and how strong is the love of Christ during their repetitive, mundane, work-a-day life are the ones who are rooted in His grace. They are the ones who are ever conscious of the name of the Lord. They are the ones who know they are able because He is able. They are the ones who revel in His presence.

But they that wait upon the LORD shall renew their strength; they shall mount up with wings as eagles; they shall run, and not be weary; and they shall walk, and not faint. (Isaiah 40:31, KJV)

Have you ever felt that you could not go on? Ever been weary? Ever been beaten up, hopeless, helpless, ridden hard and put up wet, alone, out of gas, drained, worried, abandoned, just plain tuckered out?

It would be easy, and not particularly wrong, for me simply to say that when you feel that way, you should just pray about it, and God will lift you up on eagles' wings, and won't life be fine and dandy then!

That answer, however, is too easy, and it is not always apparent to our human, tired eyes. We pray, and we say that we rely on God, and our bodies still get tired, or sick, or both. We do everything right, and then someone else figuratively punches us in the stomach and knocks the wind out of us. We move forward, doing what we feel is God's will as best we can, and then our pastor announcing he is leaving because God has called him elsewhere, or our job is eliminated, or our child quits college to play the marimba for a traveling mariachi band. We wonder why God did not let us in on the plan.

You see, I do not think the promise for strength of Isaiah 40 is based on prayer, or right living, or even necessarily seeking God's will as best we can.

This promise is based on waiting. But be careful with the scripture here, because the promise is not based on waiting for God's answers to our prayers so that we can better know His will. No. This promise is premised not on waiting for God's answers but on waiting for God.

I think the secret to strength is based on understanding our place in God's world. He is holy. We are not. He is wholly holy. Have you not known? Have you not heard that this Lord, the Creator of heaven and earth, does not faint, and is not weary? It is He who gives power to the faint and strength to them who have no might.

Too often, we say our prayers, telling God how sorry we are for previous failures and how we will do better. Then we get up and start trying, on our own, to do better. There is something missing there. Sooner or later, we realize that we messed up before because of our own weakness. Eventually, it dawns on us that we are weak and tired, and that wind gets taken from our sails through no fault of our own – and that we are powerless to bring back the wind.

Then, we have two choices. We can conclude that we are helpless victims of the storms of life and the busy-ness of our schedules, and we can then effectively fold our tents with the resigned determination to do the best we can; or we can conclude that we are children of the God who calms the storms of life and who can put the wind back in our sails. We figure out that doing the best we can is not nearly good enough. So we stop. We just quit pursuing our own vainglory. We wait on the Lord.

He renews our strength in His time. We find ourselves riding the air as if on eagles' wings. We run and are not weary. We walk and do not faint.

It is a miracle of divine proportion that the only holy thing in the universe cares enough about us to renew us. It is a mystery of equal proportion that we do not care enough to let Him.

Are you tired? Quit trying to do better.

Just stop.

Wait on the Lord.

For He is present. He has given us Himself. His presence renews.

There is another powerful reason that God's presence is so critical to the disciple's walk of faith. It is found as we contemplate what Jesus meant – and what He did not say – when He first spoke those words to Peter, Andrew, James, and John, "Leave your nets and follow me." As with many of God's commands, this one is quite clear on what is to be abandoned but not so plain about where to go next.

Or how about Abraham? There was no question where he was to leave but less clarity about where he would end up. It is true over and over again in scripture – for every Jonah who is directed to a specific Nineveh, there are a dozen like Moses (get out of Egypt), Balaam (do not go to the king of Moab), Paul (who never got to Spain), Matthew (leave your booth), the rich young ruler (sell all you have), and Shadrach (do not bow down to the king) who have an unknown calling, who are told what not to do without getting a solid direction on what to do next. In every instance, the promise is only that the Promiser is going before and leaving a trail. He knows where He is leading you. He has a plan whether it is shared with you or not.

Rarely is there a promise of a given destination or prize. Instead, we get generic terms like "promised land" and "whatsoever thy hand findeth to do." Is there a promise in there?

Yes. Inherent in the command "Follow me" is the assurance that He will be there to be followed. No one can mean "follow me" without being ahead on the path that He intends us to take, whether it leads through the dark, by the sea, or on our everyday road.

Walking in faith means going even when there is no stated destination, no clear objective, no exit strategy. Jesus did not come to show us the end but instead to make straight the path. Jesus is not the target; He is the way. Our assurance comes not from a vision of the final rest but rather with the illumination of His footprints in the sand through which we are now to walk.

What does your heart desire? Faith no longer desires the luxuries offered by this world but instead is satisfied with the company of the Giver. Faith looks not for the pot of gold but instead cherishes the rainbow as we follow through the valley, across the mountains, into the future that disappears answerless over the next rise marked only by royal footprints. Those divine tracks eventually lead all of us to Calvary; thank God they do not stop there.

Listen to the call on the gentle wind. It is not a call to meet Him. As you discover that following, not arriving, is what your heart now desires, don't expect the will of God for your life to be announced to you in the form of a destination. It is a call to follow wherever He leads. You will not walk alone.

To a youth, of course, being alone can mean having no support for your Christian beliefs among your peers when you are outside of your church youth group. It can mean facing issues that are new to you and that you are certain have never before been dealt with by anybody. It can mean being dumped by a prom date or getting the infamous "let's just be friends" speech. Alone can mean "nobody understands me." Alone can mean struggling with feelings, emotions, and actions that you are certain leave you away from God in the dark of the night.

To adults, is it so different? Being alone can mean leaving our church, entering our weekday lives, and knowing of no Christian support. Alone can mean facing issues that are new to us and with which we are certain nobody has ever before dealt. It can mean divorce. It can mean death. It can mean abandonment, isolation. It can mean "nobody understands me." Alone can mean struggling with feelings, actions, thoughts, sins, and temptations that you are certain leave you against God in the dark of the night.

But we are not alone. As parents, raising children is a team sport. I am not in it alone. As church family members, none of us has to house refugees or share the gospel by ourselves. We have many ways of working, and we walk on different pathways, but we aim together. In Him, we are whole.

When we fail, whether it is in the dark of the night or in the piercing sight of the world, we find Him waiting on the shore, stirring the coals of the fire and asking, "Do you love me?" Even when we run from Him, to the far side of the sea or to the big city with our inheritance, we are not alone. He has made us, and He knows us. He knows when we sit and when we rise. Where can we go from His presence?

I have a friend who writes songs. In struggling with how to relate to his 13-year-old son, he wrote a song to his boy that includes the line "it helps me to remember that I am not the only one who loves you." You see, my friend is not alone.

Are you sick? Tired? Poor? Confused? Defeated? You are not alone.

Are you struggling with how God can possibly use you? You are not alone.

Are you running from God, hoping He will not see into your soul and through your charades? Give it up. You are not alone.

Are you desperately waiting for someone to notice you?

Are you suffering? Did you wake up this morning and realize that everyone in your family is suddenly ill, that your joints do not work like they used to, that your dreams are not coming true, that time may prevent you from fixing all of your past failures? You are not alone.

Adam the disobedient, you are not alone. Hagar the outcast, you are not alone. Moses the stutterer, Esther the Jewess, Jonah the rebellious, Ruth the widowed, Ezekiel the confused, Habakkuk the distraught, John the Baptist in the wilderness with your honey and locusts, Jesus the tempted, John the exiled, Peter the denier, woman caught in adultery, woman at the well, crucified thief,

Paul in prison, Mary Magdalene, woman who just reaches out to touch His cloak… you are not alone.

O God, remind us. We are not alone.

That promise, that reminder, is not what the legal world could call consideration. What it is is presence; it is love. The One who is present with us is love. The world does not understand, but we do because we have His presence.

We certainly should offer consideration to God. We bring worship that He loves. We can offer praise that the Psalmist says He will inhabit. We can commit our lives to service and love and adoration to Him. But since we are who we are and God is who God is, whatever we bring to God will be overwhelmed by the "consideration" that we receive – Himself. He is with us. He is present. Always.

Let's celebrate His presence.

The Lord Helps Those...

But because of his great love for us, God, who is rich in mercy, made us alive with Christ even when we were dead in transgressions—it is by grace you have been saved. (Ephesians 2:4-5, NIV)

The law I practice in my career formulates the "rules" - the boundaries, if you will, for how American society and commerce operate. The goal of almost everyone I know is to maximize his or her personal success (however he or she defines "success") by working hard, mixing in a little luck, and placing himself or herself in a position to benefit from the workings and opportunities of what we call America.

As a lawyer, I find myself helping clients to help themselves, either by planning for personal financial futures, contracting for business-building deals, or minimizing liability. Down and out individuals try hard to "rehabilitate" and turn their lives around. Companies search for the new strategy or product and try to find a "workout" to escape the apparent doom on the horizon while hoping their stock price rises.

My clients know that you have to spend money to make money, and they know that laziness gets them nowhere. In business and in law, the watchword seems to be that the Lord helps those who help themselves.

That is business and law. It is also the world of sports, where those who practice longest and work the hardest generally find themselves wearing the rings. It is the truth of education, where study, class attendance, and extra time spent on term papers translate into higher grades. It most definitely characterizes the world of music, where practice may not make perfect, but practice makes permanent. Even the prodigy has to play the instrument for hours on end – the more work, the better the product. You help yourself, and you end up with a better result.

It is business. It is law. It is education and sports and music and better bridge playing and cooking and mastery of my teenager's XBox. But, the maxim that "the Lord helps those who help themselves" is not the gospel, and it does not work for our spiritual lives.

It is in the simple truths of the gospel that the most profound understanding of God is found, and it is by that same simplicity that we are often the most confused.

The simplicity of the gospel is that saving grace is not of our own doing. We do not earn it, work for it, keep some part of a bargain to get it, or even seek it out. We were not born into grace. We did not deserve it because we were good. We do not deserve it now. Instead, we accept what is done for us and given to us by another.

OK, simple enough. That is Vacation Bible School 101.

How easily we forget.

While we were yet sinners, Christ died for us. When we were dead in our transgressions, God made us alive with Christ. Do you get it? Not after we had turned our lives around and were ready for some religion. Not because we had finally hit rock bottom and turned our gaze upward. Not because we searched through the world's offerings and ultimately came to the place where we recognized that proverbial "God-shaped void" within us.

Instead, it is because we were on sinking sand. God saw us walking straight to hell in the depths of sin and shame. Our hearts were clouded in shades of night.

God cannot stand that. He loves us too much.

God, who created us and who could wipe us out and create a whole new species, chose not to stay seated on His throne while we wandered and stumbled. Instead, He entered our mire and our filth and our chaos and lifted us out. He picked that time, as we were at our worst and falling even further, to come to us and call our names. He did not wait until some time when we would finally turn to Him at the end of our ropes.

No. He called long before we heard.

It is the most basic story of the gospel. From "Adam, where are you?" to the prodigal son's waiting father, from Nathan's reprimand of David to Paul's sermon on the Acropolis, from Billy Sunday to Billy Graham to the prison chaplain to the local FCA meeting. Perhaps to you also, talking with a friend. The Word of God has gone forth into the heart of the world's unseeking, uninterested sinner and lifted out people just like you and me.

I remember my college pastor, Ron Durham, for a great many things, but one paragraph of one sermon he preached will always be my first and best memory of him. Ron said one Sunday, in a sermon entitled "Behind the

Eight Ball," that we should examine the phrase "the Lord helps those who help themselves." I remember Ron standing just a bit on his tiptoes and raising his voice ever so slightly to point out that that phrase is NOT scriptural. The point of the gospel, Ron told us, is that God helps those who CANNOT help themselves!

The miracle of salvation involves God's mercy and grace. There is no question that the work of the Holy Spirit in stirring our hearts through conviction of sin is indispensable. The singular event of the cross, with the nails and His pierced brow, set a new standard for the provision of grace to His people.

Before all of that though, before the act of love and forgiveness that lifted us to our higher plain, there was the call. Before we heard, while we remained sinners – sworn enemies of the one holy God – He came in lovingkindness to us. The credit that goes to us for the call is exactly zero. I do not believe the call is irresistible, and I believe that we have the free choice to reject it; but the fact that we play a role in the process in no way diminishes the grace that calls in the first place. He lifted me up to hear a call that had come before I heard or cared.

We have all been there. We've all been shrouded in shades of night. We have all felt the heat of the kitchen, open hostility, or our own sin and shame and wanderings that leave God no alternative but to chastise us. Our testimony is that we don't stay in the heat of the hostility, or the night. God won't let us.

For in the day of trouble He will conceal me in His tabernacle; in the secret place of His tent He will hide me; He will lift me up on a rock. (Psalm 27:5, NAS)

In lovingkindness, He comes to reclaim our souls from the depths into which we have plunged. The power of the almighty Creator of the universe is channeled through the tenderness of the hand of the Christ as we are lifted to places that we had not, only moments before, even been able to imagine.

Of course, being humans in a sinful world, we do not always find ourselves in those beyond-imagination places; but as Christians, we can look ahead with hope because we can look back to that time when He lifted us. Perhaps your lowest depth was a time of rebellion. Maybe it was the sting of death, or divorce, or disease, or betrayal. Maybe you found yourself in the miry bog of poverty or abuse or loneliness. Perhaps it was the pit of depression. Whatever it was, you can look back now and see how He lifted you out of it and placed you by His side.

As we feel Him lifting us, as we remember when He has lifted us before, we cannot help but do what we as Christians do best. Our testimony grows to worship as we lift our voices in joy and thanksgiving.

O praise His name, He lifted me!

God helps those who cannot help themselves.

Coming Home

The initial acceptance of Christ, when we learn that we have a Savior who died for us and who has demonstrated the power to give us eternal life, is a singularly incredible experience. For Christians, though, the wonder of God's forgiveness and saving power does not end with our salvation. Even as saved humans, we are still human. As Paul explains in the seventh chapter of Romans, our old natures are constantly warring with our newly created selves. Too often, we are tempted by and onto the paths of sin, and we wander far away. For some of us, our testimony of our post-conversion transgressions is much worse than the description of our sinful lives before we were saved. Our spiritual selves become weak and haggard. We need revival – whether it is in a tent for two weeks or simply on our knees in the darkness of our own room.

But when he came to his senses, he said, "How many of my father's hired men have more than enough bread, but I am dying here with hunger! I will get up and go to my father…." (Luke 15:17-18, NAS)

Fortunately, God is not through with us when we come out of the baptismal pool. The process of continuing redemption and forgiveness – and yes, revival – is what I think Jesus would call "coming home." The father in Jesus's parable called it time to kill the fatted calf; the prodigal son in the story knew it was time to celebrate the unthinkable goodness of his loving, waiting father. My friend and Christian brother, David Danner, called it "Beginning Again."

In the words of songwriter Don Francisco, God is continuing to call to us: "Although you've chosen darkness… I'll be running out to meet you…. There's no sin you can imagine that is stronger than my love. And it's all yours if you'll come home again to me."

In response to those words from our loving, waiting, forgiving Father, our souls are revived again, and we say, "Lord, I'm coming home."

THOUGHTS ABOUT THE CHURCH

Mavis

Two are better than one, because they have a good return for their work: if one falls down, his friend can help him up. But pity the man who falls and has no one to help him up! (Ecclesiastes 4:9-10, NIV)

It was not to be expected that Mavis and I should become fast friends. When we first met, she was a single woman in her sixties, and I was married and in my late twenties. She had been a member of our church for decades; I had been a member for less than two years. Her closest friends were from a completely different circle from mine.

One day I got a call from a member of the church's nominating committee, asking me to be on the Long Range Planning Committee chaired by Mavis. I naively said "yes." About a month later, I got a call asking me to serve as Vice-Chairman; my naiveté had not abated, and I jumped in.

Every week for the next two plus years, I worked closely with Mavis. Yes, we worked with the committee as a whole, and there is not a person on that committee who did not make great sacrifice of time and energy. But for every meeting of the entire committee, Mavis and I met three or four times – often with our pastor and often alone – in a conference room outside our pastor's office.

My point is not to discuss church committee work. My point is to talk about Mavis.

Some knew her as a co-worker, a boss, a subordinate, a minister. Some knew her as a church member, choir member, committee member. A few knew her as one of their prime encouragers. I knew her as many of those things, but most of all I knew her as my friend.

In 1996, Mavis died. I remember her funeral well. Mavis was eulogized as a writer, a master of the English language, a humorist, a traveler, an exemplary Christian, and a friend.

So why am I asking you to take your precious time to read about a dear lady whom you did not know? Because I think we all have something to learn from my memories of Mavis. In remembering Mavis, I have discovered three things in my walk with God that are of universal application.

The first thing to share with you is that we should all build our lives around being a friend. Mavis knew what it was to be a friend. As I said, there was no demographic reason that Mavis and I should have been friends. Certainly serving together on a church committee does not always engender close friendships!

Yet Mavis was my friend. She got to know me very well. She was interested in my insights and my point of view. She learned what my strengths were as quickly as she could, and then she counted on me to exercise those strengths.

Mavis was kind to me. I have no doubt that my inexperience and my too-quick decisions often led me in the wrong directions, but Mavis listened to me, tried to understand me, and was simply nice to me.

Mavis was generous. It became a tradition, when she returned from one of her many international ventures, for her to bring back some sort of odd knickknack for my children.

Mavis looked to find me and my family on Sundays and Wednesdays around the church building. When she found us, she always invested some of herself in our lives. She cared about me. She was my friend.

We can learn so much. Get to know people. Be kind. Be generous. Invest yourself in the lives of those around you. It is a legacy that will not be forgotten.

A second thing I learned from Mavis concerns prayer. You see, when Mavis got sick, some of her dearest friends gathered around her. They anointed her with oil and prayed that she would be healed.

Mavis died anyway.

That is a hard lesson. Some months later, I heard a Nazarene minister from a great church in our city tell an amazingly moving story of his deliverance from disease even as his family planned his funeral. We hear those stories, and we read in the scriptures about miraculous healings. Then we read James tell us to do just what was done with Mavis, promising that the prayer of the righteous man has great effect and that the sick will rise up and will be healed.

Mavis died anyway.

You see, that taught me a lot about prayer. Because I know no one more righteous than Mavis, or than Josephine and Norma and Gene and the other friends who prayed over her, and I absolutely believe the scriptures. That means that I must believe that Mavis rose up and was healed.

We have a lot to learn about healing. Healing is obviously not always what we think it is, nor is it always what we think we need, and it is often not what we say we want. In fact, we have a lot to learn about a lot of God's promises. We only get to see a tiny corner of the great work that God is creating, and our little human minds do not comprehend how the whole masterpiece fits together. We simply have the wrong point of view. Having very little idea what the whole picture looks like, we certainly do not understand what is good and what is bad in each situation. I think that Mavis knew that, and I have no doubt that she is healed, without pain and singing her heart out right now, joining the angels on her favorite hymn, "All the Way My Saviour Leads Me."

Yes, even at the end, Mavis taught me about prayer. She taught me that we ask in faith as best we understand the scripture, what God has taught us, and our own situation, and then we leave the ball in God's court. He hears and answers. He heals, and we rise up.

That became quite a message for me six months later when the deacons at another Baptist church gathered to pray and anoint. This time, the patient was Bob Lynch, and God healed again, quickly, ending months of pain and misery and sadness. Mavis had helped prepare me for the passing - the ultimate healing - of my father-in-law.

The last thing I learned from my memories of Mavis that I want to share with you is a word of warning. In the summer, Mavis was in one of our local medical centers for surgery. I went to see her, only to learn that she had already left the hospital and was home, doing quite well. In fact, I saw her at church less than a month later.

Tragically, Mavis's quick recovery was not long lasting, and she was soon home in bed, doing very poorly.

I did not go see her.

I do not really know why. I think honestly that I did not understand how sick she was. I also think that I was busy, doing very worthwhile things, many of which Mavis herself had been involved with six months earlier. I also think that I did not take the time to find out enough about my friend, because all I had to do was ask.

Mavis never asked for me to come. When I heard from her, she was always asking about me, my work, and my family. She never talked about herself. I took advantage of that. When it came time for me to think of Mavis, I failed.

I tell you that not so you will be upset with me or to provide myself some sort of helpful catharsis through a lingering emotional crisis – I am doing fine. I share this warning with you because I learned from Mavis to take advantage of opportunities. Find your friends. Invest in them. Be close enough to know when you are needed. Don't miss opportunities that you will regret the rest of your life.

I do not think Mavis is mad at me. If she is reading this I know what she is doing. She is a little irritated that I talked about the prayer of the "righteous man" instead of the "righteous person," and she is smiling and reading carefully for any grammatical or punctuation errors. Her being mad is not the point. My missed opportunity with Mavis is a positive if I make it that. I will not miss the next time that I need to make that phone call, send that email, or take the time for that visit.

You should not miss it either. You too can learn from Mavis. Be a friend. Invest in the lives that surround you. Pray faithfully and be open-minded enough to recognize the hand of God, even if He is working in a way that you did not expect or really even want. Take advantage of the opportunities that come your way, for some of them will not come again.

Mavis – here's to you. I thank my God in every remembrance of you, always with joy in every prayer. I thank my God for your fellowship in the gospel. And I am sure that He who began a good work in you will bring it to completion in the day of Christ.

Partnerships and Associations

Blest be the tie that binds our hearts in Christian love. The fellowship of kindred minds is like to Thine above.

The law recognizes an amazing number of ways for people to be joined together. People can be husband and wife, partners, joint venturers, conspirators, stockholders, directors, incorporators, members, adoptive parents, buyers and sellers, a joint enterprise, contracting parties, agents, employers and employees, joint tortfeasors, privies, or fellow servants.

We in the church are bound together. In the eyes of the law, some churches are actually corporations, and most of the rest are "unincorporated associations." That kind of legal joinder has no real significance to us. What has eternal importance is that we are "God's chosen people."

Therefore, as God's chosen people, holy and dearly loved, clothe yourselves with compassion, kindness, humility, gentleness and patience. Bear with each other and forgive whatever grievances you may have against one another. Forgive as the Lord forgave you. And over all these virtues put on love, which binds them all together in perfect unity. (Colossians 3:12-15, NIV)

What is the "tie that binds our hearts?" Why do we Christians share our mutual woes? Why is it that we know that though we may part asunder, we shall see one another again?

The easy answer, the one that springs to our Sunday School-trained minds, is "our love." We answer that these things are true because we love one another. I beg to differ.

Our love for each other is not what binds us together but rather what results because we are bound together. The Holy Spirit, through His immortal and infallible love, is the tie that binds our hearts. Once we are bound together, we then demonstrate the Christian love that sheds the sympathizing tear.

Why is this distinction important? Does the order of where our love falls into play really matter?

I think it does. Too often, when times get difficult, or when relationships are strained, or when the state of our fellowship is not all it should be, we turn to each other to fix things. We confidently put our trust in our love for one another and our horizontal personal commitments – which are undoubtedly very strong - to pull us through the tough times. We convince ourselves that we can love each other through anything.

The problem is that we cannot always do it. We are all human beings, and the people whom we love and on whom we are counting to love us through the storms of life are also human beings. Human beings can and will let you down.

The Holy Spirit of God, though, cannot, does not, and will not let us down. He cannot fail. The Spirit of the one who died for us and lives in us will continue to bind us together as we look to Him as that blessed tie. Our fellowship, the koinonia which is inexplicable to those who do not know Jesus Christ, must revolve around our vertical relationship with the Holy Spirit. For where two or three of us are gathered in His name, there will He be also.

Christ died for us, lives in us, and binds us together. Therefore, recognizing the binding fellowship given to us by our Lord as people who are holy and dearly loved, let us clothe ourselves with compassion, kindness, humility, gentleness, and patience. Let us forgive each other, not because of who we are, but because He has forgiven us. Then, because of His presence in our lives and because He first loved us and now binds us together, on top of all these things, we put on love.

Bound together with love, we then turn outward, to see what God has for us to do. We read that we are the body of Christ, that we are His hands and His eyes. He touches the world through us.

I don't get it. If I were God (and aren't we all glad I am not!), I would have done it differently. It makes no sense to me.

Why use us? Why on earth - if you were the Creator and sustainer of everything, the one who laid the foundations of the earth while the morning stars sang together for joy, the one who endowed the heart with wisdom and gave understanding to the mind, the one who provides food for the ravens - would you choose to work through us? After all, we are weak, we are small, we are not all that smart, we are clearly often not very committed, and we are sinful.

If I were God, I would have the angels do it. I would use my most powerful, swiftest, craftiest creatures to carry out my will.

Or better yet, I would do it myself. I would walk on the earth and touch the sick and the lame, and I would teach everyone about myself and my ways. Everything would be great then.

Right up until the time somebody planned a crucifixion.

I guess maybe there are some pretty good reasons why God works through us.

The first and maybe most important reason was seen all around my church for ten days or so after Hurricane Katrina struck, when nearly two hundred refugees found shelter, more food than they could eat, job counseling and opportunity, and the love of God poured out to them by church members volunteering hours upon hours. Our pastor led in this effort, telling us that we would do it simply because "it is what Christ is doing." When Christ works through us, His people come together in our own renewal of commitment, of koinonia, of service. I heard many of my friends and co-laborers talk about the importance to them – not to the evacuees, but to them as church members – of getting the opportunity to be the compassion and the kindness of Christ.

I think another reason is that God made people to reach people. Prophets spoke the words of God, but if the truth is not lived out in our lives, words are just words. Creation tells the glory of God, but many, many people neither glorify Him nor give thanks to Him when they see His invisible qualities revealed in nature. But when we deliver a touch, His love changes humanity.

There is another, maybe more subtle reason. I believe in the power of the church. There is nothing that the church, when it is on its A-game, cannot do for God. And the church is at its best only when it is fully functioning as the body of Christ. Of course Christ is doing it Himself. He uses His hands to touch the desperate, for we are the hands of Christ. It is His voice that calms the melee, for He sings through us. It is His empathy, His compassion that reaches out to the hurting, for we have the mind of Christ.

Now you are the body of Christ, and each one of you is a part of it. I do not mean to minimize the power of Jesus, for there is no question that He could choose to do these things without us. Still, I do not see Him working to touch the world except through His church. I am not ready to say I understand it, but honesty compels me to report that for many reasons of His own choosing, Christ uses no hands but ours.

Take my hands and let them move at the impulse of thy love.

Take my feet and let them be swift and beautiful for Thee.

Take my voice and let me sing always, only for my king.

We have not incorporated, married, signed a partnership agreement, bought a condo together, or co-signed a note. What we have done is let Him join us in an eternal union we call the "church."

Blest be the tie that binds our hearts!

Reminders

You will be glad (and maybe surprised!) to know that we lawyers have a requirement placed upon us by the licensing boards to attend a certain number of hours each year of what is called CLE - Continuing Legal Education. We go to seminars or read materials on the Internet or listen to tapes, all with the idea of maintaining expertise and keeping awareness of ethical duties at the forefront of our minds.

The CLE that I find the most rewarding is often not about a new case that has radically changed the law but rather a refresher course on some basic concepts of procedure or evidence that I first learned in school. What keeps me on my toes and feeling good about being a lawyer is often being reminded of what I learned first that got me off on the right foot.

That is not all that different from what I like best about worship.

Restore to me the joy of your salvation and grant me a willing spirit, to sustain me. (Psalm 51:12, NIV)

Usually, when we think of Psalm 51, we center on confession, repentance, and forgiveness. That makes sense because David penned this Psalm after being confronted by Nathan with his own sin. For a moment, allow me license to focus on a different slant of this Psalm.

The functions of worship are varied, and they are perhaps different to various people. Still, there can be little disagreement that we hold worship services for some reasons on which we all agree: to exalt the majestic name of our God; to praise Jesus Christ our Savior; to revive the body of Christ to return to the streets of the world for evangelism and ministry; to provide opportunity for public professions of faith; to learn God's vision for us and study what God has told us and is telling us; and to allow expression of that amazing *koinonia* that only those of us indwelt by the Holy Spirit can understand and share.

As I age, and as I continue to experience more of the divergent hardships and disappointments that life throws at us, I am becoming convinced of another purpose for worship: to remind.

It is sad but true that many adults, having weathered far too many storms and having lost far too many battles, simply are not expecting, or even particularly desiring, to find a place of peace and joy and rest. When we were enthusiastic and idealistic teenagers, the joy of our salvation and abundant life were very real and alluring concepts. Today, many of us are out of the joy business altogether, choosing instead to get the kids bathed and in bed in time to have thirty minutes to sit in front of the TV before getting back up to finish chores and go to sleep.

Life sometimes leaves us with little time for mystery or expectation. Our churches are full of people who are barely making it on a good day and are suffering desperately on many other days. Our Christian family, like everyone else, faces disease, unfairness, untimely death, and scores of other devastations. The long-ago fervor with which we approached our budding discipleship is replaced by a distant acknowledgment of God and a daily prayer for simple survival.

Worship becomes a unique event. It is the only thing that can remind us of what was once a matter of enthusiasm and focus, because if we do not get that reminder from worship, we are not going to get it anywhere else. Consider it continuing education for the saved. Worship should be the place where we see our joy restored. The worship leader takes on the combined role of storyteller, historian, and matchmaker. The one sitting in the pew enduring the storm *du jour* needs to be reminded of the power and the promise in her personal relationship with her maker, and worship can rekindle that relationship with the memories of why she accepted Christ in the first place. The joy of her salvation can be restored.

Perhaps worship leaders first need to take the time to remind themselves of the joy of their own salvation, their very strength. The words of David need to be foremost: "Praise the Lord, O my soul, and forget not all His benefits." (Psalm 103:2) Before leading us in worship, perhaps the leaders need to reflect on the Holy Spirit and His fruit that He bears in all of us. Leaders need to meditate, for a moment, on His amazing willingness to create in us clean hearts and to renew right spirits within us.

Then, worship will begin to remind worshipers of the source of peace... remind them of the goodness that is theirs... remind them that that He upholds them as they teach transgressors His ways... remind them to cast their burdens on Him... remind them of the reality – not a silly youthful ideal -that is God... remind them of of Jonah's words from the belly of the fish: "When my life was ebbing away, I remembered you, LORD, and my prayer rose to you, to your holy temple.... Salvation comes from the LORD...." (Jonah 2:7-10, NIV)

Get your continuing education. Sometimes, take the time to learn something new and "cutting edge" about your religion and your walk with God, but sometimes allow yourself a refresher course in what got you off on the right foot. Let your worship always remind you and those around you of the goodness and the promises of God, and let your joy be restored.

Restless Spirit – The U2 Church Search

In 1987, international sensation pop band U2, fronted by singer Bono, released its LP (a large vinyl disk of recorded music used in the days before iPods) called "The Joshua Tree." Perhaps the most popular song on that album, one that Bono often called "a kind of gospel song with a restless spirit," is the hit "I Still Haven't Found What I'm Looking For." Ambiguously speaking simultaneously to spiritual journey, romantic mishap, and life's enigmatic quest for purpose, the lyrics address choices made, options experimented with, and fulfillment missed. Despite the number of doors opened and experiences tried, Bono mournfully sings, "I still haven't found what I'm looking for."

This chapter is not a music review, nor is it an attempt to analyze the spirituality of a self-professed Irish Catholic rock band. The lyrics do warrant mention, however, in a wholly different light – the phenomenon of the twenty-first century church-search.

We all know them. They are the church-searchers. The church-searchers are not seekers. As we have come to define them, "seekers" are those unsaved souls who feel a real emptiness – the "God-sized void" – in their lives and are seeking an answer. For the seeker, a variety of churches exist to provide the style and presentation necessary to help find the answer, and I applaud that. The Great Commission demands of us that we teach and baptize all, and the Lord's invitation remains open to seekers through many different styles of Christian worship and evangelism.

Unlike seekers, the church-searchers are Christians, or at least they believe they are Christians. They are not seeking a savior, but they are clearly searching for something. They may spend time in a small, traditional mainline church. They may move to a megachurch, usually one with a conservative evangelical bent. Often, they flow to a non-denominational "community church." Whether such churches are actually affiliated with a denomination is rarely relevant to the church-searcher; the sign in front and the website do not display "Baptist" or "Presbyterian," and the church-searcher does not really care.

What seems to be prevalent about the church-searchers is that they still haven't found what they are looking for.

Why?

I want to make a radical suggestion. Perhaps the problem is not that the churches are failing to offer what the church-searchers are looking for. Perhaps the fault lies with churches that are leading the church-searchers to look for the wrong thing.

It is interesting to examine the statements of "purpose," "mission," or "vision" that many churches publish. Here are some actual statements I found on the web (with the names deleted to protect the guilty):

"_____ Church exists to bring all people into a fully devoted relationship with Jesus Christ by discovering and meeting their needs."

"Our goal at _____ Church is to promote and encourage wholehearted enjoyment of God, our families, each other and those who are still looking for Jesus."

"_____ Church exists in order to meet people at their point of need and enable them to become all that God had in mind when He made them."

Should a church be a safe, comfortable, inviting place for a seeker? Without doubt. Should a church strive, as a primary goal, to meet the needs of its own? No, it should not.

First, the church is the body of Christ, and whatever else Christ was and is about, it was and is not primarily about meeting His body's own needs. Churches' purposes range from worship to discipleship, from evangelism to ministry. And while fellowship and inreach are certainly valuable by-products of a healthy, loving church, for them to become primary goals is to turn the church's focus inward. The dying world, except for the brave seeker who will take the initiative to come through our doors, goes on dying.

Second, a diverse group of individuals will have needs too numerous to be met by an organizational church on a consistent basis. No church can successfully provide day care, aerobics, divorce recovery, Bible study for twenty-something single women, "sandwich generation" caregiver assistance, youth choir, marriage counseling, job placement, women's shelter, and Christmas crafts, without running the risk of omitting racquetball, crisis pregnancy support, FCA, senior adult cafeteria clubs, and couples' doctrinal study. More to the point, the church that is focused on trying to meet all these needs for its members has precious little – in terms of time and resources – for things like ministering to the poor, mission work in the projects around the corner or around the world, polishing a worship experience in which the Father is exalted, and yes, preparing a message for the seeker.

Third, styles change. Methods change. The church that seems to provide what the church-searcher needs today will be doing something different in six months. Personal testimonies give way to acoustic guitars and bell bottoms. In turn comes drama, which is replaced with rock bands, and then come movie clips, popcorn, and Starbucks. Even if the style works for a while, it is likely the church-searcher will see things change and again find himself or herself saying, "I still haven't found what I'm looking for."

Fourth, none of us is perfect. We have bad days, bad weeks, bad years. Suddenly, even if our church has only gotten better at meeting our needs, our own selfishness and our own personal crises blind us to what the church is offering. We leave a service unhappy because we never tuned in to start with, having been caught up in our own pain, failure, illness, or whatever. We find ourselves not "getting anything out of it" when we go to church. Staying home begins to look a lot more profitable.

Finally, and most importantly, we Christians must not be primarily concerned with what our church offers us. Not because all human institutions will ultimately fail to please us all the time – they surely will fail – but rather because Jesus calls us to something much more important than that. He calls us to be His arms, hugging the abandoned child and the widow. He calls us to be His eyes, seeing needs in the dark places. He calls us to be His ears, hearing the cries of the hungry and misguided. He calls us to be His feet, going to the beggar and to the CEO, neither of whom is likely to come to us. He calls us to look not inward but outward, not towards meeting our needs but towards sacrifice of our needs so that others might be touched. He calls us to walk where He walks, among the harlots and the lepers and the Pharisees and the crosses.

I am not against seeker-sensitive churches. I have good friends called by God to pastor several of them, and such churches are a part of His grand mosaic, bringing the message to some who will not hear it elsewhere.

I am not against church programs aimed at the membership. My family and I take advantage of them and will continue to do so.

I understand the church-search. I spent my teenage years in a dynamic church that prioritized a youth group with its own pastor, who fed and nurtured me because he and the church focused on kids like me. I spent my university years in the largest church college department in the city where my denomination's largest university is located, and my "college church" unashamedly ministered to me and my cohorts. I spent the first dozen years of my married life in one of America's most historic churches, where ordained ministers make up more than

10% of the congregation, and where I was taught and groomed and allowed to flourish.

I know, therefore, what it is like to be in a church that meets my needs. I have also been in a church that does not provide what I need. It is a good church striving to follow Jesus but one that does not have the resources or the inclination to meet my personal whims or even to build a worship service that is likely to speak to me deeply on a regular basis. I understand the temptation to say "I'm not getting anything out of it," to move on, to continue the church-search.

Yes, I believe there are times when it is appropriate to leave your church. Churches can move so far away from what an individual believer understands God's role for her to be that she needs to disengage and find a place where she can serve as God would have her serve. Some churches change radically, whether through the call of a new pastor or simply by radical internal shifts, and some members cannot in good conscience serve God under those circumstances. Being a devoted disciple who changes church membership in order to continue to follow God's call on your life is a horse of a different color from the church-searchers I am describing.

That I understand the motivation of the church-searcher is not to say it is right. At some point, I have to conclude that as long as I am looking for my own needs to be met, my restless spirit will eventually cry out, "I still haven't found what I'm looking for."

When I see my church as my opportunity to serve Him and serve others, to love God and love people, to worship Him and confess my own failings, it is then that I find what I am looking for. God will meet me there. He meets my true needs – to serve, to love, to worship, to confess. He enables me to disciple, to train, to evangelize, to minister, and yes, even to fellowship.

The fault lies not with the church-searcher, at least not primarily. The fault lies with the churches that offer shallow self-indulgence and popular quick fixes. Christians will not remain comfortable in seeking self, because He Himself indwells us, and He will not be comfortable with our seeking self. The church search focused on meeting the searcher's needs can lead to nothing but a restless spirit. It is up to the church, therefore, to refocus, lead, remind, model sacrifice, and cast a vision that goes beyond the members' needs and touches a world that needs Jesus Christ. Then, and only then, will His Holy Spirit calm our restless spirit. Then, and only then, will we find what we are looking for.

What It Means To Be God's People

There are times in life when we are so filled with God's goodness, forgiveness, wonder, and glory that we are struck with our own inadequacy. There is no way that we, with our human inarticulateness and our limited imaginations, can ever hope to praise our Creator appropriately. To those of us raised on the great hymns, a way to voice this inadequacy comes from words we have long ago set to heart: O for a thousand tongues, instead of our one, to sing our great Redeemer's praise!

We are not the only ones to feel that we cannot say it all. The old hymn reminds us that God is so wonderful that the half of it has never been told. One of contemporary Christian music's finest hours is the duet of Sandi Patty and Larnelle Harris, not finding our words to be adequate, instead proclaiming God to be "more than amazing, more than marvelous, more than miraculous, more than wonderful."

Even those who physically walked with our Lord shared the same response to the holiness and grandeur of Christ. The apostle John concludes his narrative of the works of Christ by saying:

Jesus did many other things as well. If every one of them were written down, I suppose that even the whole world would not have room for the books that would be written. (John 21:25, NIV)

To me, responding to and solving this dilemma of incomplete individual praise is the crowning purpose for our joining together as God's people. It is not that our corporate worship can completely match the glories of our God and king, nor can we truly explain what it means for His blood to avail for us. Yet, as we gather and lift our collective voices, our "thousand tongues," and as the Holy Spirit joins us and assists us to proclaim the wonders of His name, I think that God smiles on us. It is that time that we come closest to true worship.

We are His chosen people, a royal priesthood, a holy nation, a people belonging to God, that we may declare the praises of Him who called us out of darkness into His wonderful light. Once we were not a people, but now we are His people. Once we had not received mercy, but now we have received mercy. God has said, "I will live with them and walk among them, and I will be their God, and they will be my people."

Certainly that privileges us. We are His. We have a citizenship in heaven and the right to call Him "Abba, Father." We can approach the throne of grace with confidence. We can ask in the name of Christ and know that He will answer. We are loved, planned for, guided, protected, healed, and given a crown of glory and honor.

Certainly, being God's people places duties upon us. We are the body of Christ, reaching with His arms and speaking with His voice. The Great Commission is a start, the fruit of the Spirit provides us tools, and the gifts of the Spirit enable us to build up the body because we are His people.

But past the privileges and the duties, there is a caution. I think that we can and often do take for granted that we are God's people, as though it were not a great gift, as though we were owed something by God, as though it is no big deal to be His.

How do we show we are taking it for granted?

One way, of course, is simply by ignoring it, by doing nothing to honor or even acknowledge Him and nothing to show the world that we are His. We don't see His work in the sunrise or in the helpful stranger, and then we don't become the helpful stranger.

Ironically, another way we take it for granted is by doing the opposite of ignoring it, by flaunting it. We throw our status before God in the face of the world, trumpeting our own righteousness and demanding that they act as we act, or at least as we say we act. In fact, we forget that we behave as we do (when we are actually living up to our own standards) precisely because, and only because, we are God's people. It is ridiculous to expect others to act that way unless they first become God's people as well. Thus, by forgetting those New Testament ideas like transformation and rebirth, we forget that we ourselves were once not His people, walking as fools, and that it is only as new creatures, His new creatures, that we are free to walk as we now do. We have forgotten what it is to be God's people.

There is another way we take being God's people for granted. It is seen at those times when we make the name of God look foolish in the eyes of the world. It is the day when we do not let certain folks step into our hallowed halls or say certain words because we might be offended. It is the times we air our dirty laundry before the prying eyes of those who do not care how legitimate the dispute is but are only looking for a reason to ridicule or ignore the work of God. It is the moment we carelessly attach our name and support to programs, television channels, and movements that are in fact not worthy of Him. It is the Sundays and the Wednesdays when we gather for worship, prayer, Bible Study, or even choir practice and offer Him anything less than our absolute best. It is then that being God's people has lost its meaning, for we are unaware of His call on us, and we are blind to the fact that we bear His name.

We are God's people. That is a wonderful, wondrous thing. It should and must color everything we do. There is no time off or down time. You must cherish it and revel in it.

Heaven above is softer blue.

Earth around is sweeter green.

Something lives in every hue

Christless eyes have never seen.

Birds with gladder songs overflow.

Flowers with deeper beauty shine.

Since I know, as now I know,

I am His, and He is mine.

Don't ever forget.

I think God who inhabits our praise, looks forward to our gathering as the people of God for worship, fellowship, and service. Let us not disappoint Him.

What Is This Thing Called Unity?

I was once asked to speak to a church prayer breakfast on "the unity of the body." I joked at the time that the host did not tell me if I was supposed to be for it or against it. Nobody laughed.

Being for unity in a church meeting is kind of like being a politician who campaigns against crime. Along with preaching against a lottery and quoting John 3:16, we can be popular in churches by speaking in favor of unity.

It is not just a church thing. It is an American thing. President Lincoln was, after all, quoting Jesus when he said, "A house divided against itself cannot stand."

Why is unity so important?

The Psalmist tells us, "How good and how pleasant it is when brothers dwell together in unity!" (Psalm 133:1, NIV) The prophet, looking toward the holy mountain of the Lord, writes that "The wolf will live with the lamb, the leopard will lie down with the goat, the calf and the lion and the yearling together; and a little child will lead them." (Isaiah 11:6, NIV) Jesus Himself prayed, "My prayer is not for them alone. I pray also for those who will believe in Me through their message, that all of them may be one, Father, just as you are in Me and I am in You." (John 17:20-21, NIV)

Paul said, "I appeal to you, brothers, in the name of our Lord Jesus Christ, that all of you agree with one another so that there will be no divisions among you and that you may be perfectly united in mind and thought." (1 Corinthians 1:10, NIV) The early church was described this way: "All the believers were one in heart and mind." (Acts 4:32, NIV) Finally, Paul writes that, "As a prisoner for the Lord, then, I urge you to live a life worthy of the calling you have received. Be completely humble and gentle; be patient, bearing with one another in love. Make every effort to keep the unity of the Spirit through the bond of peace. There is one body and one Spirit—just as you were called to one hope when you were called – one Lord, one faith, one baptism; one God and Father of all, who is over all and through all and in all." (Ephesians 4:1-6, NIV)

Central to the faith of the Old Testament Israelites was the *Shema*, the truth: "Hear O Israel, the Lord your God is one Lord." Because God is one, one set of laws applied to both Israelites and foreigners. We see the ideal marriage expressed as "one flesh." The selfishness of Ananias and Sapphira, those who would separate Gentiles from the Jews, the prejudice toward Greek widows, the insidiousness of the Judaizers – all these things threatened the unity of the New Testament church and are forcefully condemned in scripture. The shared experience of Christ as Lord reflected in the singleness of baptism and the joint sharing of the Lord's Supper, our shared sense of mission, the shared suffering, and the love we share for each other are all bolstered by and reflected in our unity.

We sang in the seventies that "we are one in the spirit, we are one in the Lord, and we pray that all unity may one day be restored, and they'll know we are Christians by our love."

That is the easy part. Like all the politicians who are against crime, we are all with Jesus and Abe Lincoln when we call for unity.

I don't think that is the message that a lot of church people need to hear. Try raising controversial issues in many churches these days, and the answers you will probably get will be striking in their uniformity: "The church cannot face that, it might divide us;" or "The unity of the church is too important for us to tackle that." I don't think a pep rally for unity is what most of our churches need.

Of course, I am for unity of the local church and of the universal church. I am for unity because our Lord was for it and because Paul preached it and because it is the only way for the church to survive. Of course, I am for unity; the question is how do we get there and how will we know biblical unity if we have it? So, at the risk of stepping on toes, which I am undoubtedly about to do, I want to bring a caution. I do not believe unity ought to be the primary goal of a healthy church, but I do believe that biblical unity will be the necessary byproduct of our discipleship if our primary goals are right. The road to unity is doubtlessly paved with godly intentions, but what do we mean by unity? How do we define it so we know we have it?

Jesus said, "Do not suppose that I have come to bring peace to the earth. I did not come to bring peace, but a sword. For I have come to turn 'a man against his father, a daughter against her mother, a daughter-in-law against her mother-in-law' – 'a man's enemies will be the members of his own household.'" (Matthew 10:34, NIV)

And yet, this same Jesus prayed that we be one, as He and the Father are one. What, then, is Jesus' unity?

Unity is not Jesus' unity when it requires uniformity.

To use an extreme example, the most unified group of human beings I can think of in modern history exists today in another part of the world. We call them Al Qaeda. They have one goal, one expression of that goal, and only one purpose. Individual differences are irrelevant if they are tolerated at all. Individual goals appear to be immaterial.

I know that is extreme, and I am not accusing anybody in the church of terrorism. My intent is to use the ridiculous to make a point – we revel in our individuality. In the church, we call that giftedness. Paul talks about the body of Christ, and in the unity of that body, we all have different roles, different looks, even different smells. Somebody has to be the foot, while somebody else is the lung. You may be a tonsil and I may be a kneecap, but we function in our differences to become one body. You know the passage:

> Now the body is not made up of one part but of many. If the foot should say, "Because I am not a hand, I do not belong to the body," it would not for that reason cease to be part of the body. And if the ear should say, "Because I am not an eye, I do not belong to the body," it would not for that reason cease to be part of the body. If the whole body were an eye, where would the sense of hearing be? If the whole body were an ear, where would the sense of smell be? But in fact God has arranged the parts in the body, every one of them, just as he wanted them to be. If they were all one part, where would the body be? As it is, there are many parts, but one body. The eye cannot say to the hand, "I don't need you!" And the head cannot say to the feet, "I don't need you!" (1 Corinthians 12:14-21, NIV)

Indeed, later in the same Ephesians passage cited earlier, Paul makes this point clear:

> "It was He who gave some to be apostles, some to be prophets, some to be evangelists, and some to be pastors and teachers, to prepare God's people for works of service, so that the body of Christ may be built up until we all reach unity in the faith and in the knowledge of the Son of God and become mature, attaining to the whole measure of the fullness of Christ. Then we will no longer be infants, tossed back and forth by the waves, and blown here and there by every wind of teaching and by the cunning and craftiness of men in their deceitful scheming. Instead, speaking the truth in love, we will in all things grow up into him who is the Head, that is, Christ. From him the whole body, joined and held together by every supporting ligament, grows and builds itself up in love, as each part does its work." (Ephesians 4:11-16, NIV)

Unity is not Jesus' unity when nobody asks questions.

Unity, as I believe Jesus meant it, as I believe the early church practiced it, as I believe Paul preached it, and certainly as the historical protestant church fathers envisioned it, welcomes questions. Yes, I know I am from a profession that exists in an adversarial system where questioning is the stock and trade. Yes, I spent four years in high school and four years in college debating competitively. Yes, I am a trained questioner. No, I am not unfairly bringing a bias to this topic.

Do you ever see Jesus rejecting questions from among His apostles? He even embraced questions from the Pharisees, but that is a different topic for another book. Among His closest followers, the same audience who heard Him pray for God to bring unity, Jesus listened to questions about withering fig trees and who would be first in the kingdom. He opened the floor Himself with questions like "Who do men say that I am?"

I find it interesting, and frankly a little disconcerting, that a large church can have a business meeting with fifty people present. No, I do not want a shouting match. Yes, I trust church committees and staffs. But does anybody have questions? Have we developed a culture where the road to unity makes the questioner shy away? I wonder.

Even more than questioning though, the proof is in the pudding. I believe that unity is not Jesus' unity when nobody ever disagrees.

Maybe you are responding to yourself, "Lyn, of course we can ask questions at our church." But I wonder about the ability to disagree freely. When a large church of apparent spiritual maturity chooses not even to consider legitimate issues because church unity may be at stake, we need to reexamine what kind of unity we have.

President John F. Kennedy said, "The unity of freedom has never relied on uniformity of opinion. "

A strong unified church can handle disagreement. Please hear me, I am not in favor of strife, discord, or anger. Nor am I promoting debate for debate's sake in the church. But somehow, we are in danger of developing a culture that says, in the name of unity, I cannot voice my disagreement. I cannot stand up and say "I disagree."

The dangers here are manifold. On a theological level, this is the issue that has driven a dagger into the heart of some of Christendom's previously most admired groups and denominations. Today, many groups find themselves led by those who have stood up and declared that members must toe the line or leave the building – you must agree or you are not welcome, you do not qualify, you are not right. Ironically, in the name of unity, those who will not suffer disagreement have caused the greatest disunity the church has ever seen.

Another danger is the possibility of continuing in our wrongness without testing it. I don't know who is right or who is wrong on all of these issues, but as long as we continue to do it as we have always done it and refuse to question and allow disagreement, we will never know if we are right or wrong. All we will know is that we are firm in our stance.

After all, there is very little difference between a path and a rut.

The biggest danger is missing a work of God. I know that God on occasion may move an entire congregations simultaneously to the same point. At least as often, I believe, God starts a movement with a few people. Perhaps it is an Amos, a Martin Luther, a Roger Williams, a few churchmen and women who are willing to stand up and say, "This is not what we should be doing anymore, not what we should be preaching, not how we should be ministering, I disagree with the church." When that disagreement is allowed, the voice of God may be heard.

There is another danger. Often, those who disagree with our tradition and our majority are wrong, but when they are not free to question or to disagree, they will leave. They do not like or understand what we are doing or why we are doing it, but when public disagreement is frowned upon in the name of unity, their options are to suffer in silence or to go somewhere else, or worse, to go nowhere at all. In the name of unity, we in the church can mirror the doctrinaire leadership that characterizes many denominations today as we unwittingly drive wedges.

I know there is a ditch on both sides of the road. If you hear what I am saying as an invitation to anarchy or as an excuse to stand up in business meeting and complain when the church administrator has decided to buy a new copy machine, then you are putting words in my mouth. The freedom to disagree, like all Christian freedoms, carries with it the responsibility to do so in Christian love and with a conscious mindfulness of the feelings of others, the work of the church staff and committees, and yes, church unity.

I do not have an agenda for any specific program. I am here to say that we should be open to the new voice, to the disagreeing opinion, without feeling threatened as a unified body. If that voice is wrong, the wisdom of the church under the leadership of the Holy Spirit will prevail. I have witnessed dozens of church meetings where there was honest, and even heated disagreement in the spirit of love and peace, and where the body spoke. After the issue is decided, the united church acts.

Unity is not Jesus' unity when the focus is wrong.

Let me begin this section with a quotation: "...[T]he unity of our people and the unity of our various nationalities - these are the basic guarantees of the sure triumph of our cause."

That quote could be heard from some pulpits I know, but it is originally from an interesting pamphlet entitled "On the Correct Handling of Contradictions Among the People" by Mao Tse Tung. Again, while the church is no closer to espousing Communism than it is to channeling Al Qaeda, we have to realize that there can be unity around the wrong thing as easily as there can be unity around the right thing.

I am using the word "focus" here not in the vision sense but in the mathematical sense. The focus of a parabola is the unmoving central point around which the curve is gathered and drawn. An ellipse's shape and size are determined by two fixed points called foci.

When the church's focus is Jesus Christ, then unity is right. When the focus is anything else, and I mean anything else, then the road to unity is wrong.

What do I mean? What other things can distract us? Well, they can certainly be bad things. If the Tower of Babel story teaches us anything, it teaches us that people who call themselves God's people but who focus on something other than God's plan- here it was their own desire to join together in unity to put themselves on the same plane as God– can have that unity destroyed when God intervenes. The Pharisees were united. The Inquisition, though carried out by government, was born of a unified effort of a church.

But the other things that can catch the focus of a church are probably not in that league. Instead, these all fall into the category of the good getting in the way of the best. Carefully, let me give some examples. Churches can focus on worship style, church growth, *koinonia*, meeting the needs of church members, providing cultural relevance, raising money, or even on unity. Yes, I am saying that unity should not be a primary goal of the church. Unity is the natural result when the primary goal, the focus of the church, is Jesus Christ, His mission, His blood, His righteousness, His love, His face. Our church should be built on one truth, the Great Confession that Jesus is the Christ, the Son of the Living God. When we all revolve around that point, we cannot help but to be in unity.

Unity is not Jesus' unity when it becomes a fortress.

Of all the dangers inherent in giving lip service to unity, the specter of "fortress church" may be the hardest to prevent for the unwary. We find ourselves building a church on a Benjamin Franklin theology: "We must all hang together, or assuredly, we will all hang separately." In the course of striving for unity, we can become completely focused on ourselves. In the name of unity, we get together for fellowship and men's prayer breakfast.

There is nothing wrong with that. We form motorcycle clubs and have departmental fellowships. Nothing wrong with those either.

Except...

Then, we decide it is time for ministry, and our first thought becomes ourselves. Let's find some senior adults in the church who need help with chores. Let's all get together and repaint the nursery. Let's look around and see what members of our church need our help.

Please hear me. I am against none of these things. I think we must help our seniors and our needy. When the nursery needs repainting, by all means let's go do it.

What I am criticizing is a church mentality that looks *first* to ourselves.

The church is the body of Christ, and whatever else Christ was and is about, it was and is not primarily about meeting His body's own needs.

If, in the name of unity, our ministry program becomes solely, or primarily aerobics, divorce recovery, caregiver assistance, job placement, volleyball, senior adult cafeteria clubs, and yes, men's prayer breakfast, we run the risk that a dying world outside our walls goes right on dying.

I have probably offended most of you with something in the last paragraph, and I have not meant to. I think that every ministry opportunity that we see should be pursued, assuming it has a viable place in the Lord's work and if we feel led by the Holy Spirit to follow it. My point is that the church bent on unity can become a fortress, taking care of its own, protecting itself from danger and division, and blind to the world around it.

Jesus calls us to something much greater than a church striving to preserve itself. He calls us to be His eyes, seeing needs in the dark places. He calls us to be His ears, hearing the cries of the hungry and of the misguided. He calls us to be His feet, going out of our fortress to the needy. He calls us to look not inward but outward, not toward meeting our needs but toward sacrifice of our needs so that others may be touched. He calls us to walk where He walks, among the harlots and the lepers and the Pharisees and the crosses.

But here is the kicker – I am indeed in favor of church unity. The church that does not require uniformity but instead celebrates its internal differences and utilizes its many gifts will be unified. The church where questions and disagreement can be voiced openly and received lovingly will be stronger as a single unit. The church focused on Jesus Christ cannot help but be unified. The church that is not a fortress but a ministering body that touches its community will be the paragon of unity.

I believe strongly that the church is biblical when it is in one accord. But I do not believe that the early church fathers got up every day agreeing with each other about every issue any more than they got up and were uniform in their choice of breakfast. If you read the scripture, you find they did not make unity their goal but instead were in one accord because they were continually praising God, continually in prayer, continually working for the purpose of the Holy Spirit. They did not cease teaching and preaching Jesus as the Christ.

Church unity is critical. But it is a byproduct of our discipleship, of our commitment to the work of Christ, of our focus on our Savior.

> *So in Christ we who are many form one body, and each member belongs to all the others.* (Romans 12:5, NIV)
>
> *There is neither Jew nor Greek, slave nor free, male nor female, for you are all one in Christ Jesus.* (Galatians 3:28, NIV)
>
> *If you have any encouragement from being united with Christ, if any comfort from his love, if any fellowship with the Spirit, if any tenderness and compassion, then make my joy complete by being like-minded, having the same love, being one in spirit and purpose. Do nothing out of selfish ambition or vain conceit, but in humility consider others better than yourselves. Each of you should look not only to your own interests, but also to the interests of others. Your attitude should be the same as that of Christ Jesus....* (Philippians 2:1-5, NIV)
>
> *Finally, all of you, live in harmony with one another.* (1 Peter 3:8, NIV)

Richard Baxter, a seventeenth century Puritan, said it this way: "In necessary things, unity; in doubtful things, liberty; in all things, charity."

May God bless us and give us unity as we follow Him in one accord.

THOUGHTS ON WITNESSING

Assessing the Witness – The Greatest Compliment

It is a critical moment. The plaintiff has testified about her injury, telling the jury how it happened (according to her) and how badly hurt she is. She has put on her best efforts to try to convince twelve of her legal "peers" to award her a lot of money – at the expense of my client. I have to win the jury over during this cross-examination, or it is going to be a very long trial.

Occasionally, that cross-exam rests on a known lie that the witness has told or on establishing some physical fact that refutes her testimony, but those cases are rare. If it were that clear, we would never have to get as far as the actual trial. Most of the time, I have to operate on how I assess the witness. Is she honest? Is she smart? Is she sincere? Does she really have anything important to say? Is she so moved by bias or self-pity that she cannot be trusted? Can she really remember what she says she can remember?

It is not just lawyers who have to assess what we hear. Every person has to make judgments about the people with whom they come into contact. If we did not, we would be giving money to every telephone solicitation and handout request.

Instead of being the lawyer, I sometimes picture myself as the witness – How would I be assessed? Would the jury like me? Would they buy what I was selling? Would they go back into that jury room and compliment me?

For a moment, I want you to think about what I consider the greatest compliment in Scripture. It is not a compliment that is given in flashy language. In fact, we are not even told that the compliment was verbalized. It is not a compliment that serves as the basis for many great Christian hymns that I know of. In fact, I do not think that I have heard even one sermon based on this verse. I am willing to bet that you have never noticed it in scripture, or if you have, you passed over it.

It has volumes to say about what results when we have an encounter with Christ. The compliment is in the fourth chapter of Acts, and the recipients are Peter and John. Before we read it we need to know the context.

I love the story of Peter. I love his story because I identify with him in so many ways. He wanted to experience things. (Remember, he was the one who walked on the water.) Despite his experiences with Christ, he let his human doubts overcome him. (Remember, he was the one who sank in the middle of his walk across the lake because he decided that what he was doing could not be done.) I want to identify with him because he was passionate about his decisions and because he had insights that were not simply based on what other men could see.

Most of all, I identify with Peter because he chickened out when the chips were down. Like me, he turned an easy opportunity to witness into a bold-faced, stone-cold, absolutely dishonest denial. Like me, he saw the face of Christ turn to him and knew that he had failed miserably, and by all appearances, unalterably. Like me, Peter needed a new start to his relationship with Christ. He was unable to right his own wrongs and return to the mission on which God had placed him.

Amazingly, of course, Jesus granted Peter that fresh start, forgiving him and commissioning him to shepherd His flock. Amazingly, Jesus grants us the same privilege. Despite our failures, inadequacies, denials, and unworthiness, when we assume that we are forgotten and deserve to be forgotten, He chooses to encounter us once more in personal relationship.

The context of the greatest compliment in scripture follows Peter's famous denial of Christ within, by my best calculations, somewhere between fifty and seventy-five days. What a wonderful two months! Christ arose, affirmed his forgiveness of Peter, commissioned Peter to feed His lambs, and then, as the third verse of the Book of Acts tells us, spent a few weeks unraveling many of the mysteries of the Kingdom of God for His chosen apostles, including Peter, before ascending into heaven. Forgiven and having encountered Christ anew, Peter preached the sermon on Pentecost with the empowering Holy Spirit newly found among the believers, and thousands of people became Christians. The church grew.

Suddenly, Scripture moves to a chance encounter with a crippled beggar on the steps of the temple. Instead of providing money to the man, Peter and John offer him the healing power of Jesus Christ, and Peter seizes upon the opportunity provided by the miraculous healing to preach another great sermon. The religious leaders throw them in jail for the evening and then have what amounts to an arraignment hearing the following morning, where Peter once again takes the opportunity to tell them what his encounter with Jesus has meant to him and what it could mean to them.

Now, that is a very long introduction to get to my point, because it is at that point that the greatest compliment in Scripture appears:

When they saw the courage of Peter and John and realized that they were unschooled, ordinary men, they were astonished and they took note that these men had been with Jesus. (Acts 4:13, NIV)

Wow. How often have you met someone and left with the clear knowledge that he or she has been with Jesus? More importantly, how often do people come away from you with the knowledge that you have been with Jesus?

Jesus told us that people know Him by us. We are the body of Christ, so the only way people see Christ is to see us.

When I was in high school, we struggled with the question put this way: If you were charged with Christianity, could you be convicted? People are looking to see the evidence, the fruit, if you will, that you have been with Jesus. Too many people in this world make valiant, but human and therefore failing, efforts to be good like Jesus without ever having had an encounter with Jesus. Let me caution you that in order to show that you have been with Jesus, you have to actually have been with Jesus.

In the first century, the believers were called Christians – "little Christs" – because people could look at them and marvel that they had been with Jesus. Today, we still bear that name.

A young soldier was once brought to Alexander the Great, having been charged with cowardice. The king asked what he was called, and the frightened voice answered "Alexander, sir." The general turned up his nose and responded simply: "Son, you change your ways, or you change your name."

May He never instruct us to change our names.

Instead, may people see us and hear us and be around us and know that, irrespective of our education or our training, we have a personal relationship with the Creator of the world. May they assess us as witnesses and know that we have been with Jesus.

The Art of the Question and Answer – Jumping through Hoops

The practice of law has many varied areas of emphasis and specialization. Mine happens to be litigation. I have been certified as a civil trial specialist. What I do best is try lawsuits.

Trials involve things like lawyer arguments and jury instructions from a judge and written documents, but the heart of every trial is the evidence that is presented from the witness stand. A "witness" is a person who has relevant knowledge about material facts, a person who knows something that the jury needs to know. The witness speaks to the jury to tell what the witness knows, and what the witness says is called "testimony." The lawyer's art is to ask the right questions in the right way at the right time and with the right intonation in order to draw out the desired testimony from the witness.

Something else I have to do in a trial is to tackle the issue of witness qualification. If the testifier is one whom I have put on the stand, it is my job to take that witness through a series of questions, to have him or her "jump through some legal hoops," in order to prove to the satisfaction of the judge and the jury that this witness is qualified to render an opinion or actually has the requisite experience to report an event. Did he see it? Could she really hear it? Does he have the expertise to give an opinion on this? Is she lying?

If I am cross-examining a witness put on by my opponent, it is often the best tactic to attempt to have the witness disqualified because the witness is not legally competent to testify. In other words, I often will make a motion based on my assertion that the opponent has not jumped through the necessary hoops to have a witness allowed to testify by the court. He couldn't see. She is not qualified. He has no meaningful experience. She is dishonest. You get the idea.

You are the light of the world. A city on a hill cannot be hidden. Neither do people light a lamp and put it under a bowl. Instead they put it on its stand, and it gives light to everyone in the house. In the same way, let your light shine before men, that they may see your good deeds and praise your Father in heaven. (Matthew 5:14-16, NIV)

President Ronald Reagan loved to refer to the Soviet Union (for you young readers, that was an enemy nation that used to exist in Europe and Asia) as "the bear out there." In the next breath, and in a grand juxtaposition (and mixed metaphor), President Reagan would talk about the United States as "the shining city on the hill." The implication was obvious. We were not a nation to be feared; rather, the U.S.A. was a beacon, a people with something to share and the willingness to share it, a place ready to let its light shine.

One of the songs that Gena and I taught our children when they were preschoolers was "This Little Light of Mine." You know, "Hide it under a bushel? NO! I'm gonna let it shine." That song is based on the words of the Master, when Jesus told those listening to Him on the mountainside to let their light shine before all people in all the earth. We take that command and sing to our children to shine, and then we say that as God's people we need to shine His light to the world's people who need the Lord. As adults, we encourage ourselves, as the children of Zion, to hasten to the fields white for the harvest.

There is an assumption being made in all of these exhortations, and it is an assumption that we often ignore. In order to be a witness, you have to have a testimony. Before you can let your light shine, you have to have a light.

We are the light of the world. This is not optional. We are not told that we should be the light of the world or that it would be neat if we tried to become the light of the world. We are the light of the world. For whatever reason, this is Christ's plan. We are it. Absent us, the children of God, the world is left in darkness. The wonder of our witness is knowing how and where to let that light shine.

One of my many jobs is "witness training." I neither script testimony for my clients and witnesses nor "coach" them through hours of practice testimony. What I do is sit down with them and talk about what it is to be a witness, what will be expected of them in court, and how to handle themselves on the stand.

Then I make sure that they and I both know what their testimony is. It would probably surprise you to learn how many potential witnesses do not know how important what they know is. They think that they should not be called to the stand because they have nothing of value or interest to say. They are almost always wrong.

"Witnessing" is one of those church words that causes many of us to thumb through the pages of the hymnal until the preacher changes the subject. We are uncomfortable because we say we do not know how to witness or we do not have the gift of evangelism or we do not want to make our unsaved friends and acquaintances uncomfortable. We think we have nothing of value or interest to say. All of our excuses miss the point. He stated that we are the light of the world as a positive statement of being (not a command or a wish). Jesus did not say we should be but that we shall be witnesses at home in our Jerusalems, in our neighboring Judaeas, in our unfriendly Samarias, and to the uttermost parts of our world. He did not tell us that we should try to become salty. He said that we are the salt of the earth. The question is whether we have lost our flavor.

The mystery of witnessing is not uncovered by theoretical apologetics grounded in doctoral dissertations. The question of "What light can I shine?" is not answered by teaching us a litany or creed; nor is the response simply to pass out tracts and parrot others' words.

The wonder of our witness is our own history. People can argue with your logic; they cannot deny your experience. It is not our duty to explain about the light to anyone. Ours is to let our light shine before all people that they may glorify the Father in heaven.

Isn't it interesting how many good churchgoers do not tell others why they go to church, or why they are Christians, or anything else about their faith? Jesus called that kind of telling being a "witness," and our churches are full of people who cannot or do not or will not be a witness to their neighbors and friends. Sometimes we are afraid to offend. Maybe it is because we do not think we know how to tell about faith, or church, or Jesus. Maybe we think we need more training. Maybe we just don't know what to say. Maybe because we think that people to whom we witness will ask us hard questions and make us work so hard to prove our case to them that it will not be worth the effort.

I think a lot of us are guilty of overcomplicating witnessing. I think we do not know the right questions or the right answers. We think that the entire testimony process is so complicated that we cannot possibly do it right.

There is an old story about a newlywed couple getting ready for a fancy homemade meal at their new apartment. The bride was busily preparing the supper when her husband noticed that she cut off what appeared to be about a quarter of a perfectly good ham. Although he did not want to embarrass his new wife, curiosity got the best of him as they finished what was a delicious meal, and he asked his wife why she had cut off the end of the ham.

Her response surprised him: "Why, that is how my mother always did it. I don't know why."

Inspired by his curiosity, she called her mother, only to hear the same thing: "Why, dear, that is how my mother always did it."

It was not until the couple, who by now were eagerly awaiting some deep, complicated family cooking secret, talked to the grandmother that the rationale became clear. Through her laughter, the grandmother's explanation could be heard: "Honey, I used to cut off the end of the ham because my pan was too short!"

Just as the young wife overcomplicated what should have been a simple recipe, I think people have doubts and insecurities about church because, perhaps fearing cross-examination, they overcomplicate it. If you are not a member or regular attender of a church, you may wonder what church is all about. Even if you are a church member, you may often ask yourself why we spend all this time, energy, and money on this thing called church.

We can overcomplicate the answer to that question and create a number of doubts and insecurities when the meaning to church is simple – it is Jesus.

If you are not a Christian, you undoubtedly have questions about Jesus – perhaps how He could be God and man at the same time – that nobody has ever been able to answer to your satisfaction. If you are a Christian, you may not be telling people about Jesus because you are afraid that there are questions out there – maybe explanations of the virgin birth or the relationship between the Son and the Holy Spirit – that you cannot answer. The reason for church becomes overcomplicated with intellectual questions and theoretical answers.

Understanding what faith is all about is much simpler than we make it. Think about a Bible story that we all know. I want you to recall a particular apostle of Jesus, the one whose name as we know it is always preceded by an adjective. You know. We do not think of "Bashful Bartholomew" or "Happy Philip," but when we talk about one disciple, we have such a name. We never simply say "Thomas." We say "Doubting Thomas." Why? Because he had questions, or at least thought he did. After Jesus had risen from the dead, He appeared to ten of the disciples, but Thomas was not there. Look at his story.

> *Now Thomas (called Didymus), one of the Twelve, was not with the disciples when Jesus came. So the other disciples told him, "We have seen the Lord!" But he said to them, "Unless I see the nail marks in his hands and put my finger where the nails were, and put my hand into his side, I will not believe it." A week later his disciples were in the house again, and Thomas was with them. Though the doors were locked, Jesus came and stood among them and said, "Peace be with you!" Then he said to Thomas, "Put your finger here; see my hands. Reach out your hand and put it into my side. Stop doubting and believe." Thomas said to him, "My Lord and my God!"* (John 20:24-28, NIV)

Thomas had all sorts of questions, hoops that had to be jumped through. Perhaps "Doubting Thomas" is not as accurate as "Intellectual Thomas." He had to think everything through, or so he thought; but the point is so much simpler.

Be very careful with the passage. In this very descriptive narrative about what happened, there is no indication that Thomas actually touched Jesus. Thomas had said that he would not believe unless all of his conditions were met, and Jesus even offered to meet those conditions. Jumping through those hoops was never required because something much more basic and important happened. Thomas saw Jesus and, without touching any wounds, fell on his knees and proclaimed, "My Lord and My God."

You see, answering all of the tricky questions was neither necessary nor important. What was sufficient for Thomas was seeing Jesus.

The same thing happened after Jesus talked to a woman at a well. He told her things about her life that no mere mortal could have known, and she knew she had met the Messiah. She ran and told her friends. They were intrigued by her story. They came to meet Jesus for themselves and soon they too were followers. Their words are enlightening:

...and they were saying to the woman, "It is no longer because of what you said that we believe, for we have heard for ourselves and know that this One is indeed the Savior of the world." (John 4:42, NAS)

What people tell you about Jesus can lead you to Him, whether they are Jesus' closest disciples or people who have just had their first experience with Christ. Once led to Him, though, you will still have more questions about Him than anyone can answer. When people meet Jesus, something happens to their souls, and their questions no longer are impediments to faith.

Jesus said, "If I be lifted up, I will draw all men to me." That has meaning about the cross and about worship, but it also has a direct meaning when we are trying to figure out what all this church stuff is all about. If you are a Christian, quit trying to answer all of the questions anyone can throw at you about Jesus; that is a losing battle. There will always be another question about whether God can make a rock so big that He cannot move it. Quit talking about Jesus – introduce people to Jesus. He can take care of the questions. If we lift Him up, He will take care of drawing people to Him.

When I am eliciting testimony in a courtroom, there a number of ways for me to get where I want to go. The theories that are out there in my profession about how to do it "right" are endless. But the bottom line is that for me to win the trial, the jury has to see what I need it to see.

Our real world "juries" must see Jesus. We need not jump through a lot of hoops to qualify ourselves to show them Jesus or be able to answer every potential cross-examination that may come our way.

We are those who have found Him. If He is your all in all, how do you translate that to those who seek Him? In the 1970s, we asked "How do you tell a hungry man about the bread of life?" Now, we turn again to those who yearn for Christ wherever they happen to have cast their lot. What can we offer them? What can we share with those who do not know what we know or have what we have?

We can show them joy – not constant happiness irrespective of what the world offers, but the joy that is in our hearts.

We can show them light – not always a lack of clouds and storms, but holy light.

What we can show them is Jesus. He is the joy of our loving hearts. It is He who sheds over the world His light.

Do not worry about trying to figure out how to witness or how to become salty or how to become a light. Tell what has happened to you. That will hold up your light, and it will light the way to Him. If you know Jesus, you are the light of the world. Just let your light shine.

One day in the nineteenth century, a custodian in a great cathedral was going about his business when a young man approached him and asked if the custodian might unlock the organ so the stranger could play. To do so would be against the rules, but there was something about the visitor that touched the worker's heart, and so he pulled out his keys and opened up the instrument. What followed was the most beautiful music he had ever heard. When the man finished playing, the custodian admiringly asked him his name.

"Oh, I am Felix Mendelssohn," the stranger replied.

As he left, the custodian thought to himself: "To think that the master was here, and I almost did not give him the key."

The gospel is not about requiring that hands be put certain places and that fingers touch certain things and that manmade conditions be met. Being a witness for Jesus Christ and an ambassador for the church is not a matter of jumping through hoops to get "qualified." People will argue with your logic, but they cannot deny your experience. Witnessing is about giving the key to the master, about lifting up Jesus and letting Him draw people to Himself.

Playing a Part in Acquiring a Pardon

Fanny J. Crosby wrote many words that we Baptists love to sing.

She also wrote some words that we sing because they are doctrinally important, whether we love to sing them or not. At least, for those of us who think about them, we may not always love to sing them. They are demanding, unselfish words that assume we are obedient and seeking to fulfill our commitments.

One of those lyrics is "Rescue the perishing, care for the dying. Snatch them in pity from sin and the grave.... Jesus is merciful. Jesus will save."

Rescue the perishing...

For God so loved the world, that He gave His only begotten Son, that whoever believes in Him should not perish, but have eternal life. (John 3:16, NAS)

Should not "perish"...

I used the thesaurus function on my computer, and the results were not pretty: "Perish... depart... expire... terminate... die." Not to be depressing, and not to focus on hellfire and brimstone, but I doubt many of us spend a lot of time thinking about the real meaning of John 3:16. People are perishing; they are dying. Their erring ways should cause us to weep. Like the Ethiopian eunuch who happened to be found along Philip's way, people need the Lord. They need to be rescued.

There are times in the career of a criminal defense lawyer that the legal training, skills, and tactics have not been enough. The client is found guilty and is sentenced to be punished. Occasionally, hopefully very rarely, there is the client who is sentenced to death. Even the best lawyers have guilty clients, and when there is conviction of guilt, the law intends for a sentence to be carried out.

It is then that the lawyer stops focusing solely on appealing the questions of law and starts seeking out and out mercy. John Grisham's *The Chamber*, Richard North Patterson's *Conviction*, and Scott Turow's *Ultimate Punishment* discuss many of the nuances and emotions involved for the lawyer in such an event. Susan Sarandon played it out for us, from the perspective of a nun, in

123

"Dead Man Walking." The advocate goes to one who can pardon, the governor in most cases, and asks for mercy for the guilty one.

In a sense, the lawyer in that instance is piloting the lifeboat. The guilty client is headed for a certain - and deserved - end unless he is rescued. Mercy - the New Testament calls it grace - is required to rescue him, for justice has already resulted in the sentence.

As the body of Christ, we operate a lifeboat service. We labor to snatch our neighbors from the jaws of death, and our Lord provides the strength for the job. We have a duty to care that our friends are dying and to bring them to Jesus. We cannot do the hard part – merciful Jesus will save – but we can lift up the fallen and tell them of Jesus, who waits for them even as they continue to slight Him. We can plead with them, and we can patiently point them in the narrow way that leads to rescue. We can, and we must, tell our perishing brothers and sisters the gospel that Jesus died and the joyful sound that Jesus saves.

Like the lawyer whose appeals have been exhausted, we still know the way to the One in whose hands mercy rests, and we can put those around us who are guilty and whose sentence is otherwise sure in touch with Him.

You have heard all this before. After ten thousand or so church services, perhaps these gospel words do not stir you any longer. You tell yourself that is OK, you are still doing your part by attending a worship service on most Sundays and bringing an occasional offering. It is easy for us to deny that our fire has been dampened. In our hearts, feelings that we need to be out rescuing lie buried, crushed by whom and what we face in the hours of living every day.

Then the loving heart of God touches us, and we too are rescued as we turn to the One who forgives when we only believe.

As the church universal, the saved children of God, Christians personify the rescued rescuers. The grace of our Father restores us as the kindness of Christ includes us once more in the amazing process of salvation. We witness the wonder of baptism as young lives join the family, and we recall the mystery of how the Lord works through us to rescue.

Remember your earnestness. Care for the dying. Find the way to take them to the mercy seat. Rescue them before they perish.

Name Dropping

Therefore also God highly exalted Him, and bestowed on Him the name which is above every name, that at the name of Jesus every knee should bow, of those who are in heaven, and on earth, and under the earth.... (Philippians 2:9-10, NAS)

Growing up and living for many years in Nashville, being a member of one of the larger churches in town, traveling, debating competitively, and practicing law, I have had many opportunities to meet (and occasionally to get to know) people whose names are known well in various circles. For example, I can drop the names of songwriters, performers, governors, senators, judges, chief executives, pastors, athletes, and professors whose names would, in the right circles, draw meaningful head nods and admiration. A few of them know (or knew) me well. I am sure that many of them do not remember me at all.

I remember with clarity the days leading up to the death of my friend Bob Mulloy. I grew up with his kids and sang in his choir and watched him lead other groups in great moments of music, and any time I sing a song of his, I remember him.

I remember David Danner's funeral. David may have been the most imaginative pianist I have ever heard. David was a great talent, a committed Christian, and, for many of us, a very good friend. From now on, whenever many of us sing a piece that David arranged or a hymn that he wrote like "Holy Is His Name" or "Jesus Is the Song," we will get the attention of the person in front of us or elbow the person next to us and point to the name "Danner" on the page and say, "I knew him.... He was my friend."

That is not so different from when I went to college and told people that I was from Nashville. Inevitably, the conversation would turn to country music, and it would take me about fifteen seconds to mention that I was a friend of Larry Gatlin. When the traveling cast of Lloyd Webber's "Phantom of the Opera" was in town, my wife Gena told everyone who would listen that she had been in school with the actor playing the Phantom's understudy. (She knows him as "Billy," even though the program referred to him as "William.") It is like times when we are reading the sports page and see the name of the high school quarterback who lives down the street.

I wonder how often, when the conversation turns to things spiritual, we are quick to point to the name of Jesus and say, "I know Him. He's my friend." We who are quick to drop names often may never really acknowledge the power of the name of the almighty Creator of the universe. While the angels themselves fall prostrate before Him, we who are saved by His grace are shy about His name.

Joshua told the people, "Consecrate yourselves, for tomorrow the LORD will do amazing things among you." (Joshua 3:5, NIV)

Let us then approach the throne of grace with confidence. . . (Hebrews 14:6, NIV)

Have you ever been so struck by a person, event, or circumstance that everything else around you literally meant nothing? It can occur in a humorous way. When Gena I still lived in Nashville, we would occasionally find ourselves walking through the mall when Reba McEntyre would step out of a local hoity-toity dress shop or Travis Tritt would be at the next table in the restaurant. All I could do was gawk, forgetting what I was doing and leaving the last sentence unfinished.

A different, and frightening, scenario with the same reaction is a day like that Tuesday morning several years ago (Can it already have been that long?), when we first understood the irony of the date 9/11 and the meaning of the name Osama bin Laden. The box score that had been so crucial minutes before was suddenly irrelevant. In either event, something happened to stop us in our tracks with our jaws hanging open and with no words able to match the experience.

In the same way, does the presence, the love, the very existence of the amazing almighty ever simply overwhelm you?

It is a pity that we walk into the company of the supreme God of the universe and do not even acknowledge His choice to share Himself and His presence with us. Instead of repeatedly asking Him to fix our latest individual brokenness and solve our current problem, we ought to be hungering with all our being for a glimpse of His power and glory. Instead of seeking a particular blessing to get us through the present crisis, we should praise the Fount of every blessing for His love, which is better than life itself.

I do not mean to scold. I do mean for us to take seriously the opportunity - the wonderful, unique, taken for granted, awe-inspiring opportunity - provided to us when we are allowed into the sanctuary of our God. While God heals our wounds and hears our smallest cries, our response to Him cannot be founded on those answered prayers as if our acknowledgment of His gifts is somehow due consideration for His goodness. No. We need our eyes opened so that we can see Him, hear His voice that calls us to Him, and proclaim to Him, "How Great Thou Art." Because of who He is, and not just because of what He has done, we need to – indeed we must – praise Him... and praise Him... and praise Him.

Today is that chance for you. Of course, every week, every day, every moment is really a chance to express your love for God, to express your praise with your heart as well as with your lips. Today, turn your whole attention to God, instead of talking and singing about God. Let the third person discussion of God become a first and second person conversation with God.

Evaluate your whole being's thirst for God. God honors that seeking. Though He is God of the universe, He is concerned with you individually. Let us stop our common cares long enough to gawk at God, just a little.

We are the chosen seed. We are ransomed from our own just deserts. Why should we wait until we get to heaven to fall at His feet and join the everlasting song?

Honor, recognize, and applaud His name. If we can proudly point out that we know the name of a good athlete or a great composer, surely we can attribute all majesty and praise to the Lord of all.

Make your name dropping worthwhile. Give it some eternal significance. I will forevermore take any opportunity I have to tell anybody who happens to have seen a piece by Mulloy or Danner that I knew them. May I also take the opportunity to tell somebody who is wondering at the works of God that I know Him.

Will you join me?

THOUGHTS ABOUT JOY

You Shall Go Out with Joy

Larry is one of my heroes. When I think of Larry, I picture joy. This successful man who throws himself into overseeing the church's nursery for newborns has found a unique place of service, one that most men would avoid like the plague. The joy of His Christian walk as he holds a baby or explains to an expectant mother how the nursery operates flows from his being.

There are many other heroes of mine whom I would describe the same way – when I think of them, I picture joy:

Eric, my dear friend and brother in Christ, who left a promising career to re-enter college in his mid-twenties because he heard and followed the call to the ministry.

Jim, my "personal pastor" and encourager, on whom I always count to remind me why we remain committed to being disciples.

Neva, who absolutely has the smile of God whenever I see her, no matter what troubles surround her and her family.

The list goes on and on.

Do you grow weary of joyful Christians? Amid the trials and frustrations and worries of your busy schedules, do you tire of those who are always able to have peace in their lives?

Are you trying to create your own joy? Do you search the world for peace? Indeed, the world cries out "Peace... peace..." but there is no peace.

God says:

I will make an everlasting covenant with you.... Seek the LORD while he may be found; call on him while he is near.... "For my thoughts are not your thoughts, neither are your ways my ways,"... As the rain and the snow come down from heaven, and do not return to it without watering the earth and making it bud and flourish, so that it yields seed for the sower and bread for the eater, so is my word that goes out from my mouth: it will not return to me empty, but will accomplish what I desire and achieve the purpose for which I sent it. You will go out in joy and be led forth in peace; the mountains and hills will burst into song before you, and all the trees of the field will clap their hands. (Isaiah 55:3, 6-12, NIV)

131

We go out with joy because we are led by a God who can do the impossible; a God who can feed five thousand with five loaves and two fish; a God who says to those who are hungry but have no money, "Come, buy, and eat;" a God who is worshiped by the very mountains and trees around us. He takes our sorrows and gives us joy in return. He trades beauty for the ashes of our lives. He fills our lives with peace that the world cannot know. He has covenanted to love us forever.

The Lord your God is in your midst, a victorious warrior. He will exult over you with joy, He will be quiet in His love, He will rejoice over you with shouts of joy. (Zephaniah 3:17, NAS)

Therefore you too now have sorrow; but I will see you again, and your heart will rejoice, and no one takes your joy away from you. (John 16:22, NAS)

. . .neither be ye sorry; for the joy of the LORD is your strength. (Nehemiah 8:10, KJV)

Joy: "Pleasure arising from a present or expected good." When we sing or praise with a voice of joy, we affirm the presence of God and the hope, the expected good that awaits us.

I once sang under a director who was very particular about how his choir should pronounce the word joy. He always said that we had to "put a little smile on the end of it." If not, the word sounds like "jaw".

I like that. It is not joy if there is not a little smile involved.

That is not to say that joy and happiness are identical. They are not. We are joyful even when we are unhappy. In fact, joy has little to do with happiness. It has everything to do with triumph. We do not have to shrink from the darkness. We have present and expected victory from our song in the night. With lovingkindness, He reveals His power as our rock and our shield. That is a present good, even in the presence of our enemies, and that brings joy.

Joy is not a feeling that we can take or leave. It comes from the Lord. It is not something that we create out of our own circumstances. The joy of the Lord is our strength. Indeed, He is rejoicing over us with joy. There is joy in heaven over one lost soul who returns.

Paul tells us not to get caught up in the things of this world, for the kingdom of God is not meat and drink, but it is righteousness and truth and joy. Jesus tells us that the kingdom of God is like a treasure hidden in a field, and when we find that treasure, we have such joy that we sell everything we have to buy that field.

When we praise the Lord with a voice of joy, we do not mean to be taken lightly. We mean to have the voice of those who understand, fully and completely, that Christ is risen, that His power is revealed in the presence of death and defeat, that our joy comes in the morning.

Joy is God's greatest gift to us and hope for us. That is hard for some to understand. Surely, they reason, God's greatest gift is eternal life or abundant life or love or healing. Yes, I agree with all of that, but I would say that those good folks are not disagreeing with me. We may articulate the greatest gift differently, but the different words all end in the same joy. Scripture tells me that the reward in eternal life is joy, not simply everlasting existence but endless joy in the presence of the Father. He has prepared His kingdom of joy for us eternally. Abundant life results in joy. He commands us to love one another for the sole purpose that our joy may be full. He Himself rejoices over us with joy.

Praise the Lord with a voice of joy. Do not be content with everyday happiness that is here momentarily and then gone with the fickleness of our feelings. Do not even be content with determined faith, which looks up in the midst of despair and knows that things will be better in the sweet by and by. Praise the Lord with a voice of joy, reflecting God's joy in us, His precious children. Sing with joy to Him who is able to keep you from falling and to present you without blemish before the presence of the glory with exceeding joy.

It is the strength of the Lord, not our struggles or the world's hollow call for "peace," that creates the difference.

You see, those irritatingly joyful Christians are not creating their own joy. Larry and Eric do not have some secret formula for their own personal use, and neither Jim nor Neva has figured out just the proper exercise to look happy at all times. Their peace does not come from their own amazing time management skills. They know that God has loved them from the start and that they have been sent out equipped with joy and peace. God, who loved those who appear to us to be impossible to love, tackles those challenges by sending us out, just as He sent out the loaves and the fish, to accomplish what He pleases.

There are still heroes among us if you look hard enough. Oh, I am not thinking about football players, movie stars, astronauts, or even soldiers, although any of them can be heroes. No, I mean the ones around us who are good, those who are good not because it will get them anything. Indeed, being good in today's world may well lose them a lot, and it will assuredly bring on heartache at times. They are good because being good is the right thing to do. They have clean hearts and right spirits. I am talking about the nurse or the neighbor, perhaps a minister, maybe even your best friend. I am talking about a wife, a mother, a Sunday School teacher, an uncle, a boss, the lady down the street. They are all heroes. You should find them. Talk to them about their joy.

Let Him use you to meet the impossible God-sized challenges ahead, and you too will go out with joy.

Restore My Joy

Restore to me the joy of your salvation. (Psalm 51:12, NIV)

I have represented several clients on an ongoing basis. My current client and employer, a huge company involved in sometimes dangerous work, gets sued often. I believe that my client strives for safety, and I know that we have a good record in court, but the practice of law is an area where yesterday does not matter. Much like the baseball pitcher whose no-hitter last week does not help him at all if this week's opponent is beating his brains out, a courtroom lawyer cannot rest on the last jury's verdict. When my client goes to court, even if we have won the last five trials, we can lose. My client can face a huge damages penalty and the condemnation of the jury and the community based on what happens now.

Fortunately, our spiritual life is not like the courtroom or the baseball field. What happened yesterday, or last week, or years ago, or whenever Christ came into our hearts and became our Lord, means everything... even if we mess up today or tomorrow... even if we strike out the next twenty times we step to the plate... even if I lose every case and all my clients go bankrupt. We are still saved. Our salvation is sure, whether we remember that or not.

There is no condemnation for those of us who are in Christ Jesus. We know that salvation comes to us by grace through faith. Since good works cannot earn salvation, bad works cannot lose salvation. We are not capable of being pulled from our Father's hand.

Unfortunately, this precious assurance can be abused, and that abuse comes from two very different angles. Some look at sin and obligation and what is right from a very human point of view and are simply unable to believe that God would let people who continually do horrible things inherit eternal life, even if they are those who once accepted Christ.

Perhaps more dangerous is the abuse of our security by acknowledging that since we are saved, that our "fire insurance is paid up," we can do as we please. We forget the wisdom of the ages and our understanding of the will of God. Knowing that we cannot lose our salvation, we leave the pathways of God and walk as fools, doing horrible things, wasting our divine inheritance, ignoring the wonderful grace of Jesus, and adopting a most unChristlike lifestyle.

I know them, and so do you. You will understand if I do not use their real names here. Randy made a profession of faith as a teen, and I am told by his friends and family that it was sincere. Randy is not a bad person now, but there is certainly no evidence of a relationship with my Lord. Curt is a Christian who has moved from one dependency to another, occasionally returning to church for an emotional "rededication," only to run once again to problems, addictions, and despair.

There are others I know who are neither out of the church nor in rehab. In fact, they regularly sit in my Sunday School class and do their best to "do church" weekly. Still, there is no joy, no intentional daily time with Christ, no evidence of a personal growing relationship with the One who assures our salvation and sustains our every breath. If they were attorneys, they would be losing cases left and right because they have forgotten a lot of what they learned.

We cannot lose our salvation – the love of God is greater than that – but we can certainly give a lot away. Jesus said that He came to give us abundant life. We can lose all touch with His abundant riches as we fail to make the most of the time He has given us on earth. Even more draining, more damaging, more heartbreaking is our lost joy. We can, and we regularly do, lose the joy of our salvation.

Once we recognize that our lifestyle is sinful, that we have no joy, that we have lost all touch with the abundance that could be ours, that our lives are doing nothing to introduce anyone else to the kingdom of God (and may in fact be keeping people from relationship with God), we have no choice but to hit our knees and cry with the Psalmist, "Have mercy on me, O God, according to thy love." The fact that we have the assurance of our ultimate salvation in no way lessens our need to be washed clean. That we are not going to hell does nothing to keep us from needing a clean heart and a right spirit renewed in us.

David (his real name) was not good. David's heart became evil and his spirit was sinful. Though a child of God, he suffered the results of his sins the rest of his life. Confronted with his multitude of wrongs, he did not pray for God to restore to him his salvation, for that was never a question. He prayed for mercy, for cleansing, and for God to restore to him the joy of his salvation.

When our lifestyle is Davidic, there is no question that we, as Christians who have placed our faith in God, are saved from condemnation for our actions. There is, however, also no question that our life is far from what it should be, and that we have lost much of what God offers us. Still, we have hope. With David, we seek once again to know joy. On our knees, we pray, "Have mercy on me, O God, and restore my joy."

Our Joy Comes in the Mourning

Thou hast turned for me my mourning into dancing; Thou hast loosed my sackcloth and girded me with gladness. (Psalm 30:11, NAS)

My friend David Danner wrote the great musical presentation called "Our Joy Comes in the Morning," in which a grand choral expression of the amazing resurrection of Jesus on Easter Sunday morning rises above the misery that must have encompassed Friday night and Saturday. What was awful for those first two days became the greatest day ever. Bad became good.

We have a secret. There is a reason we choose to gather as a family together and magnify the name of one who is invisible, one who is but a footnote in the lives of so many around us, one whose very existence is ignored by our neighbors.

The secret of our family is that what was bad has become good.

Everything about the gospel is tied up in that simple idea. Our sin is erased by forgiveness. Our failings are covered by His grace. Our fears are answered by His power. Our humanness is lost in His love. Our wanderings end with His seeking and finding us.

Frederick Buechner writes about this in *Telling the Truth: The Gospel as Comedy, Tragedy, and Fairy Tale* when he says that before the truth is good news, it is simply news. Before the wonder of forgiveness, there is only the horrible emptiness of sin.

What was bad has become good. What was sour has become fresh. What was lost has been found. What was night has become day. What was anger, for but a moment, has become favor.

At Easter, we see it best. As the prophet foretold, as Jesus Himself tried to make clear to His disciples, His dying would become His rising. Mourning gives way to morning.

And He shall be as the light of the morning, when the sun riseth, even a morning without clouds. (2 Samuel 23:4, KJV)

Joy comes in the morning for the Son rises.

The night was long. The closeness of the Last Supper had been overcome by images... bloody sweat, a treacherous kiss, soldiers, Barabbas, "what is truth?" scourging, denial, thorns, "I thirst," darkness, "My God, why have you forsaken me,? earthquake, running, hiding, shame, empty night.

But joy comes in the morning. A stone is rolled away. There is a figure in white. It is the light of the morning, when the Son rises.

The night is unexpected. The memory of your run through the fields of your life is swallowed by pain, age, disease. Your body will not do what you tell it to do.

But joy comes in the morning, when the Son rises.

The night is hard. Your salvation experience, the thrill of worship, the satisfaction of service, and the closeness of prayer are distant reminiscences, barely glimpsed through the cloak of your own sin, laziness, busyness, and struggle to hold your place in a world that cares nothing for such memories. When the finger is finally pointed at you, you join David in pleading, "Restore to me the joy of my salvation."

And joy comes in the morning, when the Son rises.

As Christmas teaches us that Jesus, the child laid in a trough in a barn, will come to us in the dirtiest of places, Easter tells us that the Son will rise when the sun rises. Night has an end. Yes, even death, for us, has an end. Weeping is for but a moment.

The secret of our family is that the most high God gives us hope - hope for each new day. He clothes us with gladness. Bad has become good. What was mourning has become dancing.

At its worst, church is a collection of little people who cannot seem to make a name for themselves in "the real world" and who use the opportunity of meeting under the guise of religion to play king for a day. At its worst, church is an excuse for the fulfillment of selfish desires under cover of the name of God.

God specializes in finding things at their worst. What was worst becomes best. Church becomes a group with a secret – the secret that we are His children, glorifying His name in one accord, praising God and having favor with all the people as the Lord adds to His church daily. Our hope is in knowing that the church of individuals seeking our own personal folly becomes, when God is added in, the church of one accord of the second chapter of Acts, church at its best. That is something about which we cannot be silent.

Where our vision may fall short is in constantly expecting only the best and thus losing all spiritual momentum when the storms begin to blow. To experience the miracle of the transformation to the best, you must first find yourself amid the worst. You must know hunger to appreciate food. Scripture is clear that we will have times of mourning. Indeed, to everything, there is a season.

The scripture is just as clear that He turns our mourning into dancing.

The play on words here is profound: We have joy in the morning, no matter the mourning of the night before. We have this joy because of Him. We do not decide to wake up happy. He comes with joy to greet our morning and our mourning.

Many of us have reason to mourn. That is OK. That is life.

It is not final. It is not hopeless. It is but a moment. What is bad will become good.

Soon, we will dance.

He has turned my mourning into dancing. Let there be great, great joy. The Son rises.

THOUGHTS ON CHRISTMAS

The Questions of Christmas

As I finish editing what is about the fourth draft of this book, I am sitting at my brother-in-law's house, surrounded by thirteen family members, the now present-free ("depresented?"... "present-less?"... "present-challenged?") Christmas tree, and remnants of torn wrapping paper that did not quite make it into the trash sacks. You see, it is December 26. "It's a Wonderful Life," "Miracle on 34th Street," "Elf," and "A Christmas Story" have all been on the TV (most of them multiple times) in the last thirty-six hours. The radio stations are still including "The Christmas Song" and "Angels We Have Heard on High" with their more normal playlist.

The incarnation is on my mind.

I hope you won't mind some Christmas thoughts in what otherwise is not a holiday book.

And Mary said to the angel, "How can this be. . .?" (Luke 1:34, NAS)

If you know many people who went to law school, then you know a lot of people who hated it. This is not a universal rule (I actually kind of liked it), but it is close. They hate it because it is hard. They hate it because it is competitive. They hate it because if they do not begin studying during Week One, they will be so hopelessly behind by the middle of the term that they can kiss a good grade good-bye.

But most of all, many people hate law school because they have to learn how to think all over again. My professors called the business of law school teaching us students "how to think like a lawyer." That meant tossing out our liberal arts training of philosophical reasoning or our business school marketing plans and placing in our minds instead a process of questioning everything until we came to a basic core value. Now, whether I am reading a casebook or talking about my child's school day, I cannot help but think through the concepts differently. I have to question.

I am trained to question. If my legal training has done nothing else, it has helped me get over pretending to know all there is to know about God and to be willing to question things.

143

When it comes to religion, we want to run from questions, as if expressing doubts and confusion or admitting that things do not make sense to us would be an indication of failure as a Christian. Instead of recognizing that our little human minds could never grasp the fullness of God or the intricacies of His plan, we want to pretend that we "get it" all the time with complete understanding.

There may be no better example than how we approach the story of the birth of Christ. Perhaps it is because we know the story by heart, but most of us never really question why God chose to enter the world as an infant in a cave outside a hamlet some distance from any metropolitan city.

We know the Christmas story so well, from the word's going out from Caesar Augustus to the days' being accomplished that she should be delivered to the swaddling clothes to the heavenly host to the flight to Egypt to Mary's keeping all of these things in her heart. It may well take you back for me to suggest that there are many "questions of Christmas."

I bet that if you begin thinking about the questions of Christmas, you will have trouble coming up with any beyond "What Child is This?" and "Do You Hear What I Hear?" After that, your questions of Christmas most likely are wondering which of the twelve days has those leaping lords and who in the world are Jeannette and Isabella.

When we cannot think of the questions, we have bypassed the mystery. We have wandered without looking for that guiding star, and we have grown too old to remember the glow of Decembers past when the child in us asked about mangers and shepherds and wondered about frankincense and myrrh.

We need to find a child within us so that we can once again open our eyes to the wonderful mysteries of God's becoming man, lest we lose all the happiness of caroling. It is a child within us who wonders why the Christ child has not even a cradle to rock or a soft pillow for His head. That our savior, shepherd, and king could come with a mission to die and become our brother, lamb, and servant is a puzzle around a mystery wrapped in a question.

We need to find the child within us to ask "Why Joseph? Why Bethlehem? Why Mary? Why trust such an ordinary girl with the One who would walk on water and deliver us all?" We would have thought that God would come with kingly crowns and regal thrones. If we take the time to ask the questions, we shrug our collective shoulders and scratch our heads. After all, to quote 4HIM, this really is a strange way to save the world. Where is His splendor?

Experiencing the time of advent and Christmas will not provide all, or even most, of the answers; nor can we find them for ourselves. Trying to understand the loving gifts of the God of the rainbow and of the manger is like trying to capture the wind on the water or measure a mother's love. The questions lead us to more questions. Yet, somehow, although we do not understand it, God's coming down to Bethlehem turns December to May and transforms a chilly morning to a smiling field ready for harvest.

We have to ask the questions. We have to find a child inside to get past the old traditions and the adult rush and the grown-up's too-quick and too-simple answers to ask the questions, to see the mystery, and to wait with faith to hear the angels still singing their song. Where is that child? How do we find a child within us?

For unto us a child is born, unto us a son is given. (Isaiah 9:6, KJV)

To find a child in you, I think you must find the Child in you. When you let that Child's peace reach you and touch you, you once again see the mystery, share the wonder of the ringing bells, and, with the angels, sing "Alleluia" to our king in the silent night.

While we cannot answer all of the questions, with the faith of that child within us we can answer the question, "Where is the Child?" He is with us. He is in us. He is our Wonderful Counselor, our Mighty God, our Everlasting Father, our Prince of Peace. To those around us at Christmas time who are asking the questions, let us tell the story of the Jesus child. He is the One who brings us light, our Savior and brother the same, our heavenly king, and the Savior of all.

There are lots of questions. Ultimately, there is but one answer:

Surely this must be God's Son.

Gloria in excelsis!

Three Christmas Poems

This chapter has nothing to do with my practice of law, but I want to share it with you anyway. There are three centuries-old Christmas poems that mean much to me. The first is not as famous as the other two, but all of them, whether set to music or read silently, have something to say about the incarnation event that needs to be said.

The first is a modern translation/paraphrase of the work of an anonymous fifteenth century poet:

I shall know Him when He comes,
Not with sound of pipe and drum,
But by the holy harmony which His coming makes in me.

He shall wear no royal robe
Or a crown of precious gold,
But He my Lord, my king, shall be always, ever there for me.

He shall not in castle warm
Live in splendor, safe from harm.
But in a manger crude he'll sleep, warmed by the breath of cows and sheep.

Come Lord Jesus, tarry not!
Find in me a resting spot.
My heart is open, come dwell within.
Let life be born in me again.

By the holy harmony which His coming makes in me,
I shall know Him when He comes.[2]

Sheep's breath.

That is one of the two phrases that stuck out to me when I first discovered this wonderful Christmas poem. At the time, though, I did not think the phrase was so wonderful. Frankly, I thought it was a little crude, a little juvenile. After all, should we really shouldn't be meditating on the Creator's being warmed by the breath of cows and sheep?

As is not unusual, I was desperately and completely wrong.

---

[2]   "I Shall Know Him When He Comes" by Douglas E. Wagner, text adapted by Charlotte Lee. Edited by Michael Perry. Choral octavo published by Hope Publishing Company (HP.A652).

I am a city boy. The language of the farm is by and large a distant memory of the stories of my grandfathers. If you are like me, the only time you ever hear the word "manger" is in relationship to the Christmas story. "And you shall find the babe wrapped in swaddling clothes, lying in a manger." "Away in a manger...." To me, regardless that I know what a manger is, I always picture it as a beautiful bed where the beautiful baby lies listening to angels sing around Him while wise men give Him gold.

The manger was a feeding trough, a crude, dirty, stinking, grungy trough where the horses, cattle, and sheep came to get their food. Lying in it, Jesus was surrounded by the sights, sounds, and smells of a barnyard. Yes, He had to put up with sheep's breath.

In God's great plan, Jesus was only practicing for the countless times that He comes to be born anew in the hearts of His people. Before Jesus comes into our lives, we have nothing worthwhile to offer. In fact, without Him, we stink! As a place for the Creator of the world to abide, our hearts are anything but warm, safe, splendid castles where a drum roll and a royal robe await Him.

Then the miracle happens. When we allow Him to come into the smelly troughs that our lives are without Him, He creates a dwelling fit for the King of Kings.

And that's where that other phrase comes in. The reason that we know Jesus has come to us – the reason we knew Him when He first came – although we cannot prove it with legal evidence or demonstrate it under a microscope, is the holy harmony which His coming makes in us.

We have a gift to share with the world. We know that Jesus has come because, instead of the sheep's breath that the world has to offer, we are filled with a holy harmony. It is up to us to share that holy harmony so that the world may know Him when He comes.

The second poem is by Christina Rosetti:

Love came down at Christmas. Love all lovely. Love divine.
Love was born at Christmas. Star and angel gave the sign.
Worship we the godhead. Love incarnate. Love divine.
Worship we our Jesus, but wherewith for sacred sign?
Love shall be our token. Love be yours and love be mine.
Love for God and all men. Love for plea and gift and sign.

Three words are key to this delicate and sometimes confusing poem.

The first word is *sign*. We look for a sign of His coming to us; star and angels gave the sign. And this shall be a sign unto you, you shall find the babe wrapped in swaddling clothes, lying in a manger.

The second word is *wherewith*. Not one we use very often, it means "with what?" I think the poet is saying this: we know how to worship God, the father, the Godhead, for He is lovely and divine. We saw the star shine and heard the angels sing. We know that this Christmas, the God of love has done something wonderful, and that something is Jesus. The question is how do we respond? How do we, who know how to worship the Father, also worship this baby? If the star and angels are His sign, what is our sign of worship, of response? Worship we our Jesus, but wherewith for sacred sign?

The poet answers her own question in the third verse. Nothing surprising here for the believer. The third word, and the answer to the "wherewith" question, is *love*. Love shall be our token. Your love and my love, love for God and love for all people. Love is His gift, and love is our sign.

"Love came down at Christmas" means that our God of love gave us a gift, but it means more than that. "Love came down at Christmas" means that our Jesus was born as love incarnate, bringing God's love to earth to walk among us, but it means more than that. It asks the question of our response, the "wherewith" question, the "what can I give Him" question. It is no accident that the one who penned these lyrics went on to pen what has become a favorite, albeit simple, children's Christmas verse: "What can I give Him, poor as I am. If I were a shepherd, I would give Him a lamb. If I were a wise man, I would do my part. But what can I give Him? Give Him my heart."

You see, that is the meaning of "Love came down at Christmas." The coming of the Christ child, the breaking through of God into our human world, was the entry point for *agape*, for the love of God, to be yours and to be mine. It was not for us to receive and feel for the first time – for the ark and the manna had already shown us His love – but for us to give. It was, and is, the instigation of a love that the world did not and cannot recognize and did not and cannot show without His coming.

What is the sign? They will know we are Christians by our love. Wherewith do we worship? With love, His love overflowing us. We love Him. We love each other. And the only reason we know to do that, the only way we know how to do that, is because Love came down at Christmas.

The third poem appears in many of our hymnals. It was written by the Latin poet Aurelius Prudentius about fourteen hundred years before it was translated into English by Baker and Neale:

Of the father's love begotten ere the worlds began to be.
He is Alpha and Omega. He the source, the ending He,
Of the things that are and have been and that future worlds will see.
Evermore and evermore!

Oh the birth, forever blessed, when the virgin, full of grace,
By the Holy Ghost conceiving, bore the Savior of our race,
And the babe, the world's redeemer, first revealed His sacred face!
Evermore and evermore!

Oh ye heights of heaven adore Him. Angel hosts His praises ring.
Powers, dominions, bow before Him and extol your God and king.
Let no tongue on earth be silent. Every voice in concert ring
Evermore and evermore!

The combination of King James language, poetic syntax that tends to take things out of our familiar subject-verb-object sentence order, and doctrine as theme can make texts like this one hard to understand. I have taken the liberty, therefore, of paraphrasing this fifth century Roman Catholic hymn, hopefully not to lessen its majesty but rather to remind myself of its message:

"He was born of and created by the Father's love before time began. He is the beginning and the end of all things that our time has ever seen or will ever see. It was a miracle, when the Father, working through His own grace and the power of the Holy Spirit, caused a virgin to have the baby, who, in growing to be the One to save us all, showed us what God is really like. Our response joins that of creation's adoration, of the angels' praise, and of the honor bestowed upon Him by the kingdoms of this world – we must worship, forever!"

There is a reason we celebrate the advent and the incarnation. The choice by Alpha and Omega to enter a manger on a night of human history in order to save puny, wayward creatures, some of whom openly scorn Him and most of whom simply ignore Him, is far beyond our understanding. We neither would nor could plan such a thing. Neither would we allow Him to work as a common tradesman, to live a life of poverty, to dine with harlots, to be spat upon, or to be killed. And we certainly could not dream of letting Him come back three days later to find His closest friends cowering in a locked room.

The plan was beyond human time and outside of human thought.

The response from those of us to whom He has revealed His sacred face is not beyond our understanding, however. The response is to celebrate, to praise. Every voice in concert ring!

Evermore. Merry Christmas.

...And a Little Child Shall Lead Them, In Peace

I have written that my legal training has taught me to question. My education and experience have trained me to keep questioning things until they make sense. I am taught to reason through the issue. I am to decide what the answer is and write a brief to convince the court that my answer is the right one.

So I have trouble with some of the great paradoxes of Scripture. It does not immediately click with me to say that if I save my life I will lose it, and that to be first I must be last. I do not want to agree that the way to victory is through taking up a cross.

And I surely do not want to look to a little child for leadership. The story of the baby in a manger brings warm fuzzy feelings but not always an assurance of the ability of that newborn to overcome every great roadblock and evil that I know is out there.

For unto us a child is born, unto us a son is given: and the government shall be upon his shoulder: and his name shall be called Wonderful, Counselor, the mighty God, the everlasting Father, the Prince of Peace. (Isaiah 9:6, KJV)

Certainly the coming of the Christ child did not end the bitter struggles of His people against the Romans occupying their homeland. Clearly the birth of the promised child has not chilled the aggression that has characterized history for the last two thousand years, just as it typified humanity for thousands of years before His coming. Though we look for it longingly, we have not yet seen even a week that could be described as world peace. War and strife continue.

Glory to God in the highest, and on earth peace, good will toward men. (Luke 2:14, KJV)

Does that ring hollow to you?

Surely the angels knew that the wars, battles, insults, lies, gossip, and anger that define humanity would continue, yet they filled the sky with glorious song. What did they understand that we may not yet grasp?

A shoot will come up from the stump of Jesse; from his roots a Branch will bear fruit. The Spirit of the LORD will rest on him— the Spirit of wisdom and of understanding, the Spirit of counsel and of power, the Spirit of knowledge and of the fear of the LORD— and he will delight in the fear of the LORD. He will not judge by what he sees with his eyes, or decide by what he hears with his ears; but with righteousness he will judge the needy, with justice he will give decisions for the poor of the earth. He will strike the earth with the rod of his mouth; with the breath of his lips he will slay the wicked. Righteousness will be his belt and faithfulness the sash around his waist. The wolf will live with the lamb, the leopard will lie down with the goat, the calf and the lion and the yearling together; and a little child will lead them. The cow will feed with the bear, their young will lie down together, and the lion will eat straw like the ox. The infant will play near the hole of the cobra, and the young child put his hand into the viper's nest. They will neither harm nor destroy on all my holy mountain, for the earth will be full of the knowledge of the LORD as the waters cover the sea. (Isaiah 11:1-9, NIV)

There is an answer here. Even for my legally-trained inquiries, there is an answer. It may not make "sense" in the way the courts would want it proven by evidence, but there is an answer here, waiting to be believed.

Perhaps the answer that the angels understood was – and is - that His coming brings peace. Not the absence of fighting – for His coming surely does not subtract from our world. No, the angels knew, as Isaiah knew, that this rod of Jesse would bring something new that would confound the wisdom of this world. God's creation, which had strained at the wrong course of things since the day the forbidden fruit was eaten, could once again rest. God was in charge, and there was once again a way. Salvation has come to the world, and all war and strife will cease one day, for those things no longer govern. This little child is the One who shall lead them, and the government is on His shoulder.

It is no more startling to see a wolf and a lamb dwelling together, or a cow and a bear feeding congenially from the same place, than it is to let a little child lead. It is ironic to us that peace should be brought by one so apparently powerless, but God's creatures – His angels, the lion, the bear, and the lamb – know the master's voice, and the world is at peace. It sees the Prince of Peace. That is why the leopard and the goat will lie down together, for they will both hear the same command from the same ruler.

The coming of the child is, in Isaiah's words, a sign for the people that His rest shall be glorious. We know that the struggles will have an end. The victory is sure. From the perspective of a people rising above the worldly tumult to see that we are on the holy mountain of the Lord, we understand that God's plan is in place. God, not evil, is in control, for He has sent His little child to lead. The lion knows it. The leopard knows it. All of His creation knows it, and is at peace.

Glory to God in the highest, and on earth, peace.

THOUGHTS ON THE NATURE OF GOD

Scientific Evidence, Expert Witnesses, and Amazing Testimony - Love Walks on Water

I used to try lawsuits for a living. I would answer Complaints, conduct discovery, take depositions, and talk to juries. I still try cases occasionally, although my job now is usually to advise and help the lawyers who are in the trenches day to day. Even now, though, perhaps the most fun I have is cross-examining an opponent expert witness.

Lawyers can find a witness to say anything, if their client's pocket is deep enough. For the right fee, "experts" will appear to offer opinions on any subject. To try to control the legitimacy of what a jury actually hears, courts follow rules of evidence about what constitutes acceptable expert testimony. The law is evolving almost weekly in this area, but the consensus seems to be that such witnesses should not be qualified as experts unless their testimony has some acceptability in the real world and represents some provable scientific theories.

I am not sure that it is possible, or right, to have a "favorite" Bible passage. The Bible is so full of richness that to single anything out may appear to minimize so much else that is essential wealth for our souls. Still, I think that I have a favorite passage. It will not surprise you. It is a story that you have read many times. I am not original in calling it my favorite:

Immediately Jesus made the disciples get into the boat and go on ahead of him to the other side, while he dismissed the crowd. After he had dismissed them, he went up on a mountainside by himself to pray. When evening came, he was there alone, but the boat was already a considerable distance from land, buffeted by the waves because the wind was against it. During the fourth watch of the night Jesus went out to them, walking on the lake. When the disciples saw him walking on the lake, they were terrified. "It's a ghost," they said, and cried out in fear. But Jesus immediately said to them: "Take courage! It is I. Don't be afraid." "Lord, if it's you," Peter replied, "tell me to come to you on the water." "Come," he said. Then Peter got down out of the boat, walked on the water and came toward Jesus. But when he saw the wind, he was afraid and, beginning to sink, cried out, "Lord, save me!" Immediately Jesus reached out his hand

and caught him. "You of little faith," he said, "why did you doubt?" And when they climbed into the boat, the wind died down. Then those who were in the boat worshiped him, saying, "Truly you are the Son of God." (Matthew 14:22-33, NIV)

The expert witness would tell us that Jesus could neither walk on water nor calm a storm with His word. The same witness would swear on a stack of studies that Peter could never take a step on the lake. But most expert witnesses also have very little understanding of what love is and what love can do.

What is happening in this story? Jesus, the Son of God, has sent His followers away from Him so that He can be alone. Suddenly, these apostles find themselves in a little boat in the middle of a big storm. Their Lord and Master is on the other side of the lake, out of sight, attending to other business. They are scared.

They have seen Him calm a storm just days or weeks before on the same lake, maybe even in the same boat. Still, they are led by a couple of fishermen who know what a storm on the little Sea of Galilee can do to such a craft, and they are scared. What Christ had done for them before is not nearly as important as what the storm can do to them now. God's love – that powerful, inexplicable, unending love – is not on their minds at the moment. Wind and waves are all around them.

Get the picture. It is not just that they are alone. The really frightening part is that Christ has sent them away into the storm. Surely Christ knows that the front is coming and the clouds are gathering. Yet He has sent them into the middle of it, and He has stayed away, and this is no ordinary storm.

Have you been there? Have you felt that everything you have ever known is being taken from you, that your world is literally about to end? Have you wondered where Jesus could be? Have you felt like the Lord was sleeping through your storm?

Notice that Jesus does not come immediately. They have just witnessed the feeding of the five thousand. Surely their faith will hold them through this time. Right? It is not until the fourth watch of the night, about 3:00 in the morning, that Jesus comes to them, and then the surprises begin. Jesus does not just come to them, but He comes walking upon the sea. Men just do not do that. Only ghosts do that, they think, so they tell each other it must be a ghost. What they should know is not that ghosts do that, but that only God does that. Do you ever miss Christ because he comes to you in a way you are not expecting? Christ does not act the way the "experts" predict.

Then Jesus speaks, and the unexpected facets of the amazing love of God continue. He does not speak to the wind and waves, as we might expect, with a majestic "Peace, be still!" Instead of commanding the storm, he addresses His disciples, saying "It is I. Do not be afraid." Instead of fixing the problem, He speaks to His children.

The love of God is often like that. We may not be surprised that Christ comes to us in our troubles, and we may not be surprised that He has answered our prayers; but it is what He says or how He answers our prayers that is unexpected. He is always present, and He always loves us. He does not always give what we want, but He is sufficient for our needs. That is love.

Another surprise is that Jesus arrives at all. You see, it had not occurred to the apostles to pray. They were apparently too busy being scared. Nowhere is it recorded in the gospels that the apostles, in the midst of their storm, cried out for God to save them or for Christ to come to them. Instead, all we know is that there was a storm, and there was Jesus.

I love Peter's response. When he sees His Lord and the miraculous power in Him, Peter forgets about the wind and the boat and the others around him. All he wants to do is walk like Jesus. Now I know that Peter does not get very far, but I love the fact that he is immediately moved to be like Jesus. I think Peter's prayer was, "Lord, if you are walking on the water, then I want to walk on water too." Jesus' answer is immediate: "Come."

Then Peter separates himself from most of us. Most of us know that God loves us and that Christ is the seat of miraculous power, and we would truly love to walk on water. I mean, really, who would not love to walk on water? Unlike me, though, Peter does more than just want to walk on water. Peter gets out of the boat. Lo and behold, he starts walking on water! As far as I can tell, this is the only place in the New Testament where a man joins Christ in performing a miracle.

Alas, Peter is so much like me. I can experience the wonders of God, new every morning, and be surprised yet again by what God is doing in my world. I can even join God, for a time, in what He is doing in the world, just as Peter joined Christ for a stroll on the waves. Sooner or later, though, and usually sooner, my gaze drifts from Jesus, and I suddenly remember that I am in a storm. I turn back to the "acceptable scientific theories" of the expert witnesses the world has to offer, and I lose my gaze on the one who is love, who walks on the water. Notice how Matthew puts it: "And when Peter came down out of the ship, he walked on the water to go to Jesus. But when he saw the wind, he was afraid, and he began to sink."

Peter does not fail because the wind gets worse or because the waves get higher or because he gets struck by lightning. Peter fails because he takes his eyes off the only thing that can keep his head above water. Maybe Peter forgets that he cannot walk on water by himself. After all, he is actually walking on water! Maybe he begins to rely on his own strength. Or maybe it is the opposite. Maybe he decides that what he is doing cannot be done, and so he quits. In either event, he takes his eyes off Christ. Don't forget that the name Peter means "rock." That is what Peter resembles as he sinks like a stone.

Once again, the surprising love of Christ – the love that made us and knows us and follows us to the far side of the sea and up with the wings of the dawn - finds Peter. Even as Peter doubts Christ and sinks, Christ does not let go of his hand. Jesus and Peter have a conversation while Peter is ... where? Either he is standing again on the water or else totally in the arms of Jesus. Then, they are back in the boat, and the storm is over.

Notice the order: first Jesus catches Peter, then He rebukes him, then He calms the storm. Jesus saves, then disciplines and teaches, then provides ultimate peace.

The love of God does not mean that the wind does not blow. Christ calls Peter to Him before He calms the storm. His presence comes first. His presence is the stuff of His love. If you have bought into the false "prosperity gospel" theology that says that once you become a Christian you will never again have any problems, then it is time to wake up and smell the coffee. The rains still come, taxes are still due, and the Braves may lose yet another World Series to those darn Yankees. Jesus does not prevent those things. In fact, our fathers still get sick and our friends get divorced, and one day we wake up to find out that our child has left home on a road that can only end up with her lying in a pig sty, wishing for a husk to eat.

How do you react in a storm? With complete faith? Do you expect His presence? What if the storm is of your own making? Do your expectations change?

The apostles were in a storm. They started out forgetting the miracles of that very day. They became scared. Then they became superstitious. Then they were awed.

The climax of this story is worship. The apostles bow in the boat with an awestruck recognition that "truly this is the Son of God." Perhaps that is where you are today. Perhaps you need to hit your knees and proclaim, maybe for the first time, that Christ is Lord. Maybe you need to accept the amazing love of God.

Do not look for the experts of the world to give you their opinions. They will never accept the premise that anyone ever walked on water, or that true selfless love exists. You have a testimony that far surpasses theirs. You have heard Him say, "It is I – don't be afraid!"

Director and King: Our Declaration of Dependence

Of course, we lawyers have to study constitutional law. Along with students of American history and government, we focus on those Articles and Amendments that make up our constitution, guaranteeing freedoms and forming the foundations of individualism on which our society is built.

I do not see how serious students of the American Constitution, especially those with an understanding of our history and of how other forms of government have been tried worldwide, can come away from their study without a deep appreciation for what that document maintains. Freedoms of speech, of press, of assembly, of free exercise of religion, and from establishment of religion undergird a document that goes on to address due process of law, freedom from state criminal law practices that were common until that time, and overreaching governmental powers. When combined with the sentiments set out in the Declaration of Independence, these freedoms and principles lead to an indefatigable enthusiasm for individualism and pride in what each one of us can do if free to do so.

And then we individualistic Americans come to the throne of Jesus and try to come up with titles for Him - "Savior," "Wonderful Counselor," "Friend," "Comforter," "Rose of Sharon," "Prince of Peace." If we are in a particularly submissive mood, perhaps "Lord."

Somehow, "King" is not an address we upper middle class Americans tend to use for Jesus very often. Perhaps our memories of fifth grade social studies (if not law school) have made "king" a bad word. Americans have no king. In fact, we fought a couple of wars over it. Perhaps it is our adult mindsets of individual rights, do it yourself Home Depot trips, and pull-yourself-up-by-your-bootstraps capitalism. We don't think we need a king, and we surely do not want one.

A slave has a different perspective. The spiritual grew out of a detestable history and drew from a self-image that yields a pose that we should all adopt. My life may be, for a time, subject to my miserable circumstances, to the whims of those who think they are my betters, to the philosophies and even religious teachings of a society that does not know my God. But I am not a citizen of this kingdom. This world is not my home. My chariot is coming. The trumpet will sound.

Our faith has found a resting place, a rock. Our world was set in order by a Creator who is uninterested in what the fad-loving ears of the day are itching to hear. He is not hindered by physical chains, political ownership, or unsound doctrine. Even the Jordan is not a challenge.

Scripture has no democratic compunction against the word *king*. "The Lord is King forever." (Psalm 10:16, KJV) "Who is this king of glory? The Lord strong and mighty." (Psalm 24:8, KJV) "I am the Lord, your Holy One, the creator of Israel, your King, thus saith the Lord...." (Isaiah 43:15-16, KJV) "Hosanna, blessed is the King of Israel, who cometh in the name of the Lord!" (John 12:13, KJV)

The spiritual "Ride on, King Jesus!" is based on the image that arises from Revelation:

I saw heaven standing open and there before me was a white horse, whose rider is called Faithful and True. With justice he judges and makes war. His eyes are like blazing fire, and on his head are many crowns. He has a name written on him that no one knows but he himself. He is dressed in a robe dipped in blood, and his name is the Word of God. The armies of heaven were following him, riding on white horses and dressed in fine linen, white and clean. Out of his mouth comes a sharp sword with which to strike down the nations. "He will rule them with an iron scepter." He treads the winepress of the fury of the wrath of God Almighty. On his robe and on his thigh he has this name written: KING OF KINGS AND LORD OF LORDS. (Revelation 19:1-16, NIV)

I am an American capitalist individualist. I made good grades in constitutional law and in my Bill of Rights class. I believe in all those things. But that is the politics and economics of this world. I cannot let it interfere with or dictate my doctrine, my spirituality, my faith. It is an honor and privilege to be subject to my king.

There is another image besides "king" that expresses our dependence on God. Let's move from the political to the dramatic, to the theatre. Let's think about a director.

I am a pretty easy audience. When I go to the theatre, I appreciate effort and ability, even if the talent level is not what those better schooled in the arts expect. But I do make one demand of the director. The author's intended story must be told. There are few things worse than going to a play when the director doesn't get it, when the actions, the interpretations, the emphases of the actors distort the intended message. When a script drawn on a grand scale is reduced by a lazy, uncreative director to paper mache' rocks and cardboard trees and bad costumes out of someone's foot locker, a script with real meaning becomes an excuse for cliché and formula because the director has no idea what the play is about.

When the director does not understand the writer, there is no sense of origin, of source. The director cannot remember the emptiness, the gloomy desolation of the blank page before there was creation, before there was an idea. Seeing only the morning of reasoned plot and characterization, the black night before of chaos and darkness is never felt, never understood. The writer's intention can become nonsense with no answer, a lock with no key.

But the exception finds what the creator intended. The outstanding director looks into the hand of the one holding the pen to understand what else is held there.

When the writer actually is the director, who as a writer really has something to say and as a director really knows how to direct, the result moves audiences and critics alike. Perhaps you have sat in a choir as Tom Fettke conducted "The Majesty and Glory of Your Name." Maybe you have heard Maya Angelou read her own poetry or listened to Billy Joel play "Piano Man." It is different. It is understood.

Consider the perfect relationship between creator and director. Stay with me here. The play is called "Life." The author is God the father, who has put all things under the feet of Christ and has given Him to be the head, the director.

You have the choice of other directors, of course. You need not choose Christ. You can produce your version of Life with a director who cheapens it with paper mache'. You can pick a director who is brilliant and accomplished and has a lot of ideas for your production but who does not know the author and will therefore lead you a different direction entirely. You might even try to direct yourself, with inevitable disaster awaiting you in a pigsty or the belly of a big fish.

You cannot, however, choose a different creator. The Origin is beyond you. The ever-living stream has laid out the course, a command that even the mountains and the waves recognize.

Your production of Life may be playing to a half-empty house, with poor reviews and no energy. You need new breath. There is hope. Find the director who knows the author, who is at the right hand of the author, who is the author, who remembers the one crucial moment because He is not bound by the strand of time.

All the world's a stage, and all of us merely players. There is a director who will give you the spirit of wisdom, enlightening your eyes, that you may know the hope of His calling and the riches of His glory. You are acting out Life. Find once again its breath.

We hold these truths to be self-evident, that all men are created equal... with certain inalienable rights... that among these are life, liberty, and the pursuit of happiness. Yes, I believe all of that, just as I embrace the freedoms of the Bill of Rights. But I have to understand that while those values must characterize how governments relate to people, they cannot overshadow how God relates to me, or how I seek to find Him.

I need a director.

I need a King.

The Certainty of the Law vs. God's Surprises

In an earlier chapter, while talking about my favorite Bible story, I alluded to a concept that has been difficult for me to embrace: we serve a God of surprises.

That is a hard thing for a lawyer to accept. I like to look up a statute, to know what the rule is and how it is applied and what is supposed to happen. If there is no regulation or statute that tells me, I can always go to the cases to see what the precedent is that the courts have developed. Law is built on predictability. I can advise a client because I can know what is supposed to happen.

God, however, works under a different set of laws. I am discovering that God has many surprises for us. Remember, He is the God who made wine flow from water pots and who walked on the water and who took up a cross instead of leading a conquering army. The God who feeds the ravens – yes, He will give us bread – but He has so much more in store for those who will look for the surprise.

The surprises of God are many, and they come to us in many different ways, but you can miss them. If you are not open to being surprised by God, you most likely will continue on your journey and not notice what new thing He has for you.

One of the great Old Testament books is the often-ignored Lamentations. Listen to these words. They serve as the basis for one of our greatest hymns.

The Lord's lovingkindnesses indeed never cease, for His compassions never fail. They are new every morning. (Lamentations 3:21-24, NAS)

Have you found anything new from God today?

I remember when I found something new and amazing from God one summer day in Colorado. His name was Matthew. I was seventeen, idealistic, and fired up for the Lord. He was in his thirties, agnostic, and excited to debate the Christian teenagers on a mission trip to his hometown. He had read about our coming in the local newspaper, and he was ready for us. To this day, Matthew remains perhaps the most well-read and articulate opponent of my faith I have ever run across. Bill and Chris and I met Matthew one afternoon, and sure enough, he engaged us in a debate.

The surprise was not that I found someone with whom to share my immature faith. The surprise was not even that I would be challenged so thoroughly. The surprise was that words came out of my mouth, and from Bill's and from Chris's, to meet (if not overwhelm) the challenges. I heard myself discussing Eastern mysticism and contrasting it to the patient, forgiving search for sinful man that characterizes the God of our faith. I knew, even as I said the words, that they were not my words. To my eleventh grade mind was being added the very power of God.

I wish I could tell you that Matthew, like the Ethiopian eunuch, asked the three of us to baptize him then and there. In fact, all he did was invite us to a bar where he was playing and singing that evening.

I do not know what has happened to Matthew, but I do know that I have been much more willing since then to see how God would surprise me when sharing opportunities have appeared. Somehow, I know that a difference was made in Matthew's life, and I think that he was surprised by his discussion with three cocky Southern boys that afternoon.

What kind of surprises does God have for you? Your surprise could be an answered prayer or a sunrise. It could be a gift for which you dared not pray, or it may well be a relationship. God may gift you with somebody who adds more to your life than you imagined possible, someone whom you had not known before, or someone who would remain, you thought, forever outside your personal sphere. The surprise may lie not in something or someone new coming into your life but rather in God's transforming something already in your life into something wonderful of which you had never before dreamed.

Maybe I am not being specific enough. Maybe you want me to paint a picture of the particular surprise that God has for you so you can go find it. I cannot do that. For one thing, in my own life, God's surprises have been varied. From words that have come to me at particularly stressful times, like the afternoon with Matthew when I had no idea how I would speak, to moments so precious that they could not have been shared with others without the presence of God. There have been such different surprises that I cannot categorize what you should expect. For another thing, God's imagination is so much greater than mine that I cannot begin to tell you how God will surprise you. On top of that, part of the nature of a surprise is that it is unpredictable.

I can point to lots of scriptural examples of God's surprises – of His mercies that are new every morning – to give you an example of what I mean:

166

- His disciples expected Him to be off praying, and Jesus decided to take a stroll across the lake.

- Sarah knew that she was well beyond child-bearing years, and she ended up being the mother of generations as numerous as the grains of sand on the beach.

- Saul headed to Damascus to help root out some more Christians, only to be struck blind by His personal encounter with the Lord.

- Goliath was surprised by the power in five smooth stones.

- One woman was surprised when Jesus called out, "Who touched me?"

- Zaccheus was surprised when Jesus looked up at him in a sycamore tree. He was surprised again when Jesus invited himself home for supper.

- Peter was surprised by more fish than his nets could hold. And by the forgiveness he found days after denying his lord. And by being told three times to "feed my lambs." And by a tongue of fire on his head. And by words coming from his mouth that could lead thousands to the baptismal waters.

As momentous as these events were, God's surprises are just as often apparently small, minor events that we can miss if we are not ready for them… The unborn child's leap of joy inside Elizabeth… the Master's wanting Mary to sit and talk instead of rushing to prepare the meal… a bush that burns but is not consumed… my law partner Gareth's day lilies, blooming just for today, when I happen to be driving by.

The hymn writer puts it this way:

Sometimes a light surprises the Christian while she sings.
It is the Lord who rises with healing in His wings.
Set free from sin and sorrow, we cheerfully can say,
Let the unknown tomorrow bring with it what it may.

We are surprised by His love. We get caught up in the many crises that surround us, whether they exist because of our sin, or because there has been another flood, or because cancer has once again struck among us. We forget, and are therefore surprised, that we serve a God who clothes us more radiantly than those lilies, and who gives us bread when we ask.

We are surprised by His constancy. We see the world around us going in directions we never anticipated, but directions that we can surely describe now as disastrous. The prophet would say that the flocks are scattered and the fig tree is bearing no fruit. We are surprised that God is still there, abiding in us and with us, still the same.

We are surprised by His compassion. He sends the sun after the rain, and He does in fact visit us with healing.

I think we are surprised because we have wandered. It is hard to be surprised by the nature of one with whom you are in constant contact. When you lose touch, you forget what He is like.

Look again at the words of this great hymn. When do we experience all of these surprises – when are we struck by His light? No, it is when we sing, when we pursue God's themes in our holy contemplation, when we confide in Him. The person who is confident in the face of the unknown is the person who is secure in the closeness of one powerful enough to handle the hidden.

When we sing this hymn, I think we will be surprised. When we continue to sing His song, I know that we will be surprised.

I cannot specify for you what your surprise will be, but there are things that I can tell you about God's surprises.

To find His surprises, you have to be walking with God. Knowing Him and abiding in His word allow us to know the truth, and the truth sets us free, and if the Son sets you free, then you are free indeed.

You cannot dictate what surprise you would like. Yes, we can ask God for anything in prayer, and yes, He often says "yes." But when we decide that we know better than God the gifts we should have, we limit to a puny human scale the heavenly possibilities that would otherwise await us.

You must be a good steward of God's surprises, just as you must exercise stewardship of all of God's gifts. The wasted day or sunrise, or the abused relationship, signals a lack of appreciation of God's marvelous imagination and generosity. When we are given something special, we must treat that gift as something special.

Perhaps the hardest thing to accept about God's surprises is that they often are outside of the rules. The surprises of God may well not fit the rules that men set up. His ways are not our ways and His thoughts are not our thoughts. Remember, if it were expected, it would not be a surprise. I do not mean that the surprise will be outside of God's rules. Paul writes very clearly that while we are called in Christ to be free, we are not to use that freedom to indulge our sinful nature. If the spirit is telling you to rob a bank or commit adultery or walk upon the downtrodden so that you can gain something you would not otherwise have or deserve, then you are listening to the wrong spirit.

So what do I mean about freedom in Christ and God's surprises and the rules of this world? I mean that our faithful God will have a new mercy for you tomorrow morning, and it may well surprise you, because you never expected it. Perhaps your peers do not expect you to have anything like that. Maybe society says that that cannot be a part of your way of life. Conceivably, some religious figure may tell you that good Christians do not go there or do that. I suggest you evaluate the source of those rules.

Many of our rules were not made with the surprises of God in mind. The rules say that you cannot walk on water and that you cannot be raised from the dead and that Jesus will not want to stop to spend time with little children. The rules say that certain people do not associate with other certain people, whether it is because of their race or their class or their marital status or their income. Fortunately, the Good Samaritan did not follow that rule. The rules say that you should not take chances so that you will not get hurt. The rules say follow the rules and you can stay in a world that is predictable and explainable and safe.

Jesus did not come to erase one bit of the law but instead to fulfill the spirit of the law. Many of our rules are well-intentioned guidelines to keep us from stepping too far, and it is always safest and easiest to stay trouble-free if we steer well clear of the boundaries. But for those willing to search for the surprises of God in the freedom that He offers, it is at the boundaries of what the world understands that God does His most exciting work. Do not be surprised that society does not want you there.

I know that what I am saying is dangerous. I run the risk of someone hearing me say that it is OK to go break all the rules.

In C.S. Lewis' masterpiece *The Lion, the Witch, and the Wardrobe*, the hero is a lion named Aslan, an allegorical Christ figure. When one of the children asks one of Aslan's faithful followers about the safety in being around such an animal, the classic reply tells us so much about the nature of Christ: "Who said anything about safe? 'Course he isn't safe. But he's good. He's the King, I tell you."[3] You see, what I am saying is dangerous because our freedom in Christ can be dangerous. You know that I am not saying that you should go break all the rules – do not go cheat on your taxes or kick the dog – but there are such blessings that await us new, each morning, if we trust totally in the good giver of that freedom.

---

[3] Lewis, C.S., The Lion, The Witch and the Wardrobe, Collier (New York:1950), Sixteenth Printing - 1975, pp. 75-76

I advise clients based on the predictability of the law that I have learned by studying statutes and precedents. Christians make plans based not on predictability of what man has set out but instead on expecting big things out of God.

How big is your God?

Where were you when I laid the earth's foundation? Tell me, if you understand. Who marked off its dimensions? Surely you know! Who stretched a measuring line across it? On what were its footings set, or who laid its cornerstone— while the morning stars sang together and all the angels shouted for joy? (Job 38:4-7, NIV)

Have you ever been in a church meeting where a new long range plan was on the agenda? Perhaps, by the time of the actual meeting, you were tired of hearing about the Long Range Plan. As the one-time vice-chairperson of my church's Long Range Planning Committee, let me assure you that you were not as tired of it as the Committee was! But being tired of hearing about it is not the issue.

The issue is whether or not an ambitious plan is worth spending any time on at all. If a church is going to try anything new, much less truly aspire to spiritual greatness and worthwhile impact on its community, there will assuredly be some negative comments about specific parts of the plan; but the most overarching concerns will deal with issues like "Who is going to do all those things?" or "How can we pay for all of that?"

Our churches are made up of people whose present resources, time, and energy are fully committed. We have only one thing left, and that is God, who waits for us with His surprises and His daily new mercies.

We could plan by looking at present giving rates and prospective growth, then taking those numbers and seeing what we could do with them. Or, we can choose to seek honestly what God would have us do and be, with the faith that if God wants it, then God will provide the means to do it.

We do not have the power to do any more, so we ask God to pour on us His power. We cannot climb any more heights with our present manpower and giving, so we must have God to set our feet on lofty places.

To make great plans, or even simply to face what the next day holds for us, we have to rely solely on God. We need Him to grant us wisdom, courage, resources, commitment, willing service, and His strength so that we will fail neither man nor our Lord. What can stop it is the feeling that "we can't do it." We cannot, but our God is a God of surprises, and He specializes in helping us do what we could not do on our own, with our own plans and in our own strength.

What makes the plans of Godly churches work is the call to our God to pour His power onto His people.

This kind of surprise of God is not for everyone. You may be at the place where you need to discover the basic gifts that God has laid out for us all – salvation, abundant life, joy, and peace – before you are ready to explore the surprising freedom of the disciple.

Maybe you are at the place where you understand about this freedom and these surprises. You are secure in His place and in His ways, and you can tell this world that its rules do not always have to be your rules. After all, His ways are not the world's ways.

If that is you, then I encourage you to look for the day lily or the floating axe head – or maybe the risen Lord – and understand that God wants to surprise you.

The First Move

But God demonstrates his own love for us in this: While we were still sinners, Christ died for us. (Romans 5:8, NIV)

One of the young lawyer's tasks is research. As law students, we are taught how to use the library as a lawyer uses it, reading strange citations and tracking down the theories that underlie decisions steeped in decades of tradition, analysis, and judgment. We start our law careers putting that training to work, climbing through musty stacks and smelly old law books to find that one old case that has the explanation.

We are taught to search until we find the answer.

It is not just the young lawyers. Older lawyers spend some time in the library too, but more often than not they have mastered the technique, and the search is not the same enormous job as it was for them earlier in their career. They know where to find the answer.

I remember when I first began working in a law firm. One of my mentors (and a name partner in the firm), Mr. Jack Robinson, pointed to all the books in our library and explained that no lawyer could hope to know all that material. Instead, explained this wise and experienced master attorney, what people pay us for is the knowhow to search out and find the answer somewhere in those books. Whether it is the student learning how to Shepardize a case for the first time or the partner returning to a beloved treatise again and again, a lawyer's stock and trade includes the ability to search until the answer is found.

Are you still searching for the answer?

Are you, like the rich young ruler who approached Jesus, still wondering what you must do to be saved?

Do you find yourself running figuratively through your life, waving your arms in a desperate attempt to get God's attention? Are you, like the young lawyer, painstakingly searching through the musty stacks of library materials of the world, certain that you will find the formula that will give you the keys to the kingdom? Are you searching for the right move to set your eternal destiny into motion?

Have you forgotten the message of the gospel?

That message, the overwhelming point of the love story that we call the Bible, is that the first move was God's. He did not wait for us to change, or to become good, or even to start a pilgrimage in search of Him. The good news is that Jesus sought us, that God came to us. While we were strangers, wandering far from His fold, He took the form of a servant and became like us. The difference between our faith and any other very serious religion that I know anything about is that God is searching for us. We need not seek Him. The scripture says that "while we were yet sinners, Christ died for us." His love is such that His precious blood was shed to rescue us, even as we remained prone to leave the God we love.

We know these words. We know that we were sinking deep in sin, deeply stained, when He lifted us. We know that we were not worthy to be called His children. We know that the wages of our sin is death.

We know the words. We act as if we did not. We go through life desperately attempting to prove our worth and our goodness and our value, as if any blessing could spring from us.

How refreshing it is to know that we do not have the burden, or the responsibility, or even the possibility, of bridging the chasm we have plowed between ourselves and God. Instead, the first move is His, and He makes that move in reaching out to us.

> Blessed be the name of the Lord from this time forth and forever. From the rising of the sun to its setting, the name of the Lord is to be praised. The Lord is high above all nations; His glory is above the heavens. Who is like the Lord our God, who is enthroned on high, who humbles Himself to behold the things that are in heaven and in the earth? (Psalm 113:2-6, NAS)

He is a God who is so great that He would have to stoop just to see the heavens and the worlds He has created. Amazingly, He does stoop, humbling himself to see the heavens and the worlds, and He lowers Himself to love the sinful, otherwise insecure persons He has created. He condescended to us once to take on the form of a servant and become like us so that He could die for us. He stoops now to be our guide and to be our friend.

I remember enough of my high school Latin to appreciate the use of the word "condescend" in the hymn and in the Psalm. "Con" comes from the word for "with," and "descend" is just what it sounds like – to come down. The dictionary defines "condescend" as voluntarily to assume equality with an inferior. My Latin tells me that when God condescends, He steps down to be with us.

What a blessing it is that we worship a God who condescended to us and who condescends to us. What security there is in knowing that His love, grace, and joy in our hearts will never end.

Acceptance is easier than acquisition. Receiving is simpler than creating. Getting is essentially effortless, especially when compared to searching.

Children understand. They come and sit on Jesus' lap and wait to see what He has for them. May we have the faith of a child.

God has made the first move. The most important step has been taken. He has condescended to find us while we were running around, searching for a way to be good and to earn a heavenly reward. We have only to join and accept in order to receive.

Do not forget that message. Quit searching for God – He has already found you.

Great Is Thy Faithfulness, Forever

Be honest. If your experience with God happened only one time and was in the far distant past and had no constancy to it, why would anybody else care?

There are probably not many of you who share with me the distinction of having your life verse from the book of Lamentations. From the manic-depressive pen of Jeremiah come these wonderful words:

I remember my affliction and my wandering, the bitterness and the gall. I well remember them, and my soul is downcast within me. Yet this I call to mind and therefore I have hope. Because of the Lord's great love, we are not consumed, for his compassions never fail. They are new every morning. Great is Your faithfulness. (Lamentations 3:19-23, NIV)

James puts it this way:

Do not be deceived, my dear brothers. Every good and perfect gift is from above, coming down from the Father of lights, in whom is no shadow of turning. (James 1:16-17, NAS)

Faithfulness is not just important in the bitterness and the gall, of course. Just ask your spouse if you are expected to demonstrate faithfulness in good times as well as in bad. So too, while we surely need God when we are in the foxholes and the hospital chapels, it is in the daily that we find our reason to be His. My testimony does not begin with a Damascus Road encounter with God, and in fact, since I was fifteen, I have had precious few of what we call "mountaintop experiences." If, unlike me, you point back to that singular time, and your witness grows out of salvation from drugs or prison or abuse or another crisis, we are different only in our beginnings. Where our testimonies converge is in the maturing process, in our daily recognition of new mercies from God that we could not see the night before, whether because of our sin or our immaturity or because God had not yet chosen to reveal them.

Where our testimonies grow strong is in looking back and seeing that He has provided all that we have needed. The Lord is my shepherd… I shall not want. Just as the earth counts on summer and winter and springtime and harvest, we rely almost unconsciously on strength for today and hope for tomorrow. The sun, moon, stars, and indeed all nature bear witness to the constancy of God. We wander; He is mercy. We sin; He is love. We fail; He pardons. We rant and rave and dissent and kick dust and strain against the goads; He is enduring peace. We chase pretty rainbows, rise on the wings of the dawn, settle on the far side of the sea, hide in the dark, find ourselves a million miles from home; His presence is there, guiding us, every single time. We change; as He has been, He ever will be.

Where theory meets reality is in human limitations. We are human, limited by our three dimensions, moving linearly forward, moment by moment, able to see only a little ways ahead.

God, however, is not confounded by limitations. Scripture tells us that he is omnipresent:

Where can I go from your Spirit? Where can I flee from your presence? (Psalm 139:7, NIV)

This faithful One is, no doubt, a God of seeming contradictions. Unseen yet heard. The first and last. My friend John Parker has written that "He was the future… He is the past."

Consider with me, for a moment, time travel. H.G. Wells wrote *The Time Machine* in 1898. Perhaps you remember Christopher Reeve and Jane Seymour in "Somewhere in Time" or TV series like "Land of the Lost" or "Star Trek." You can go online to the website called "Time Travel for Beginners." If you are brave, you can read Stephen Hawking and learn about quantum tunneling and quark theory.

John Parker has challenged us a step further than omnipresence with his words. He was the future. He is the past. God is omnitemporal.

God created everything. That means He created time. He is greater than and not limited by His creation. That means He is outside of time, unencumbered by yesterdays or "next times." God does not ever have to say, "I wish I had done that," and for us to speak of God with time words like before or already – "Did God know I was going to do that before I did it" or "Does God already know who our next pastor will be?" – is an attempt to bridle the Creator with the restraints that bind only His creatures.

Maybe this illustration works for you: In a canoe on a river, I pass first an apple orchard, then an open field, then a pine forest, then a bridge, then a village. From the orchard, I can see the field, but I cannot see further. Once I get to the bridge, I can never see the orchard or the field again. You, however, in your hot air balloon, see the orchard, the field, the forest, the bridge, and the village at the same time. They are all happening for you at once because you are not constrained by the river or the boat. You are above it all.

He was the future. He is the past.

Fortunately, the gospel is not chaos theory. Our holy, supernatural balloonist is forever faithful and true. There is nowhere better to leave our burdens, place our hope, or direct our questions about the future.

Do not let lazy twenty-first century language hinder your understanding of the great biblical idea of "faithfulness." God is not a committed spouse, a dependable soldier, a loyal friend, or a Saint Bernard. He is, and was, and will be (at least as our temporally linear minds can contemplate Him) mercy and peace and love and pardon and guidance and cheer and presence and ten thousand other things beside. He is, every single day, opening new blessings of opportunity and challenge and beauty. He is Father in every excellent sense of that word.

If you struggle with witnessing, think on these so-familiar words. You have a testimony. It is daily. All you have needed His hand has provided. If you look, you see new mercies every morning. He never changes, because He simply is.

Great is Thy faithfulness.

God Has Prospered Us

And he continued to seek God in the days of Zechariah, who had understanding through the vision of God; and as long as he sought the Lord, God prospered him. (2 Chronicles 26:5, NAS)

As I write these words, our church is preparing to call a new pastor after an "interim period" of seventeen months. I am excited about the new pastor. No, I do not know yet who it is. Judging by the scuttlebutt in the hallways, I may be the only person on the planet who does not know, but I do not know who it will be.

But I am excited because I do know that God has prospered us.

A step of faith is an interesting exercise. We can talk about the clichés of walking by faith, not by sight; or of jumping off the board, knowing that our Father is waiting in the water below to catch us and keep us safe. Clichés only go so far. Waiting seventeen months on a search conducted by ten other people is more than a cliché – it is an exercise in faith.

One step of faith has been to continue for those seventeen months on the road that we believe God has for us, a road that we have followed through more supply preachers than we can count or remember, through wondering and rumors about who might be the new pastor, and through our own failures to lead ourselves as we ought. Yet we have continued, and God has prospered.

Another step of faith has been to believe that God will protect and provide. Patience and prayer are not virtues that come easily to a dynamic people who want a position filled immediately, if not sooner. Our men and women, old and young, have, by and large, waited and trusted and prayed. God has prospered.

Now we prepare to take yet another step of faith. It is not one we take fearfully or carelessly. God has prospered us during our times without a shepherd, just as He has prospered us during the tenure of every man who has ever filled the role of pastor of our church. We know that God intends for us to draw from the wells of salvation, and we believe that the messenger of His peace and His truth is coming to us to show us the way.

Where are you now? Are you searching for what God will bring you? Are you anticipating? Or are you suffering?

Can you look around and notice that God has prospered you?

I will lift up my eyes to the mountains; from whence shall my help come? My help comes from the Lord, who made heaven and earth. He will not allow your foot to slip; He who keeps you will not slumber. Behold, He who keeps Israel will neither slumber nor sleep. (Psalm 121:1-4, NAS)

The Psalmist is not subtle. Our Lord who watches over us does not slumber. He does not sleep.

The beauty of this Psalm is that in the classical lines of the Psalmist's description of the majesty of God, reigning over us from on high in His Elysian fields, is set this simple, childlike truth: God does not go to sleep. Not only is he omnipresent, omnipotent, and omniscient, he is always awake. Children intuitively understand that about God. We should too.

We should understand it when we face grief. When we languish in the dread, loss, defeat, illness, and death, our God is not ill or dead. He is never even asleep. Despite our grief, He is there to quicken and inspire us with His tireless presence and with His endless watchfulness.

We should also understand it when we need help. We lift up our eyes to the hills from which comes our help; our help comes from the Lord, who made heaven and earth. Behold! The One watching over Israel slumbers not nor sleeps.

We should understand this simple truth when the storms of life blow. Even though we have chosen to leave Christ on the shore while we attempt to sail the great seas alone, He does not sleep. He sees the wind and waves even before we cry out to Him, and He walks across the water to where we are, floundering in the storm. He speaks peace, and there is peace.

We should understand that when we wake up in fear in the middle of the night, He is not asleep. When the fiercest giants this world has to offer are haughtily matched against us in all our puniness, He is not asleep.

If I rise on the wings of the dawn or settle on the far side of the sea, He is there, awake and watching over me.

Perhaps there is subtlety in this message. It is not subtle that God is always awake. After all, He is God. The nuances in the message lie in the fact that the God who is constantly awake chooses to spend His wakefulness watching over His people. Within the great, complicated, classical lines that describe God and His majestic glory is the simple, childlike I. The one who slumbers not nor sleeps is watching over me. I can rest amid the nightmares. I can fell the Goliaths in my way. When I lift up my eyes to the hills, my help truly comes from the Lord. He does not sleep – He is too busy caring for me.

Where sin abounded, there did grace abound all the more. (Romans 5:20, NAS)

- When Adam and Eve knew they were naked, God sent clothes
- When Cain went into the Land of Nod, God sent a mark.
- When Isaac lay bound under the knife, God sent a ram.
- When Joseph lay in a pit, God sent Egyptian traders.
- When the Red Sea blocked the way, God sent a big wind.
- When the city walls were too high, God sent trumpets.
- When the spies were found out, God sent a harlot.
- When there was nothing left for Ruth, God sent a kinsman-redeemer.
- Where there was a nine-foot enemy, God sent five smooth stones.
- When the wall had to be rebuilt, God sent the king's cupbearer.
- For such a time as this, God sent Esther.
- When the greatest wisdom became a chasing of the wind, God sent His love.
- When the fiery furnace glowed, God sent Himself.
- When the wayward seafarer was tossed overboard, God sent a big hungry fish.
- When the flocks were scattered and there were no grapes on the vine, God sent a song.
- When the crowd was too deep, God sent four friends with shovels and a mat.
- When the crowd was too tall, God sent a sycamore tree.
- When the lawyers asked hard questions, God sent simple profound stories.
- When the waves crashed, God sent a message of "Peace. Be still."
- When the Damascus Road led to persecution, God sent a bright light.
- And, at just the right time, God sent His son.

So don't act so shocked when God enters your storm. When you stumble, God lifts you up. James tells us that He gives more grace.

When death itself arrives, God sends victory.

In my weakness, He is made strong.

It is the step of faith to know that God has been with you before and that He thus will be with you again. It is faith to understand that I AM means that God is now, and that you are not left with simply what God did for you "back then."

Praise the Lord, for He has prospered us. Trust the Lord, for He will prosper us again.

Fortuitous Transfers and the Greatest Gift

And now I will show you the most excellent way... Love is patient, love is kind. It does not envy, it does not boast, it is not proud. It is not rude, it is not self-seeking, it is not easily angered, it keeps no record of wrongs. Love does not delight in evil but rejoices with the truth. It always protects, always trusts, always hopes, always perseveres. Love never fails. (1 Corinthians 12:31; 13:4-8, NIV)

Whoever does not love does not know God, because God is love. (1 John 4:8, NIV)

It probably is not hard for you to believe that we lawyers can get so caught up in using big words and doing our best to sound impressive that we actually have coined the phrase "fortuitous transfers." Would you believe that law schools actually have entire courses with that title? Recently I had a law clerk of mine tell me that she was going to be taking "Fort" next semester!

For people living in the real world (that is all of you who do not have to live with us lawyers), there is no such thing as a "fortuitous transfer;" there is just a gift, and it is a simple concept. We are given what we do not earn or deserve. That is the gospel.

Somewhere during our church lives, usually in Vacation Bible School or maybe in junior high Sunday School, we learn that 1st Corinthians 13 is "The Love Chapter." We read it and begin to hear the attributes of true love.

Always kind, patient, not selfish or rude. Eager to forgive. Bears all things. Believes all things. Hopes all things. Endures all things.

The next time a lot of us really think about the Love Chapter is during our wedding ceremony, where we hear that we are embarking on a lifelong commitment to being long-suffering, not puffed up, not keeping a record of wrongs, taking no pleasure in evil, not seeking our own, always trusting, rejoicing in the truth.

I think that, paradoxically, the Love Chapter can become a downer. We get started reading about "love" (or "charity" for you King James fans), and by the time we get to "envieth not," we have decided that there is no way we can measure up. We catch ourselves being easily provoked by relatively minor problems at home, and we decide that the Love Chapter is a nice goal, but it has very little place in real life.

I like to look at this chapter differently. Paul writes of *agape*, that almost indefinable something which is only really explained to me by the apostle John in his first letter. In exhorting us to display *agape* for each other, John writes that God is *agape* – God is love. John explains that the *agape* about which Paul writes is embodied in God himself.

This "Love Chapter," then, which describes the greatest gift we have been given or could possibly be given, becomes not an unreachable aspiration destined only to frustrate us, but instead is a description of God. In that context, the greatest gift is not an abstract, indefinable, warm, and fuzzy feeling. The greatest gift is God. We have a whole new list of reasons to worship our amazing God.

Though we speak with tongues of angels and give our goods to others and know as much as prophets, what good is that if we do not have God in our lives?

God is always kind and patient, neither jealous nor boastful nor rude. God is neither selfish nor conceited. God releases all resentment and takes no pleasure in the wrong. God finds truth delightful always. God is not easily offended, but God is eager to forgive. God is always trusting, always hoping, always enduring.

> *O LORD, you have searched me and you know me. You know when I sit and when I rise; you perceive my thoughts from afar. You discern my going out and my lying down; you are familiar with all my ways. Before a word is on my tongue you know it completely, O LORD.* (Psalm 139:1-4, NIV)

> *"Come, see a man who told me everything I ever did. Could this be the Christ?"* (John 4:29, NIV)

To me, perhaps the greatest wonder of God's relationship with me is not simply that He saved me, or even that He is willing to forgive my innumerable failings on a daily, or even hourly, basis.

No, the most amazing thing about God is that He, unlike anyone or anything else in the world, can see me as I am, and He still loves me. He is not limited in His view of me to the Sunday School teacher or softball player or deacon or writer or father or husband or lawyer or coach or play director or any other role that I am fulfilling at a given moment. He is not limited to the perspective of my parents or my teachers or my partners or my readers. He is not even held within the boundaries of what I choose to reveal to Him in my most honest of prayerful confessions. He, and He alone, can see me as I am. He loves me anyway.

God created me and everything around me, everything I see and the worlds of which I have no knowledge. He is truly the king, and His status as king calls for our worship. But His status as king is not mysterious. In fact, it is the thing about Him that makes the most sense. The heavens tell the world His glory and our souls have a God-shaped void that is seeking a king to follow. We intuitively understand that God is a powerful king.

The mystery is that the one who made me and knows me as I am gives me perfect love. He cleanses my life of transgressions. The God who leads like a shepherd reveals how much He cares by dying for me and by constantly keeping my heart strong and free. The one who truly knows me does not see my falling, my failing, my too-frequent disrespect for His simple wishes as a reason to toss me on the ash heap. Instead, He uses his almighty power to change me. Biblical writers say that he restores me. In today's world of support groups, counseling, and renewals, we might say that he brings recovery to me.

After I am changed, after my soul has been restored, after the blood of Jesus has washed away my sins, He continues to bless me and to keep me. I am clean. The world continues to see me fulfilling my many different roles, and they, and you, no doubt continue to see my failings and my faults.

God can see me, not as I was, not as the world sees me, but as He made me – as I am, clean and forgiven. And He loves me. That is a mystery, a miraculous mystery. He alone can see me as I am.

Oh what is man that You are mindful of Him? … You have made him a little lower than the angels and put him in charge of all creation. (Psalm 8:4-5, NAS)

One of my very favorite verses comes from the little book of Zephaniah.

The Lord your God is with you; He is mighty to save. He will take great delight in you, He will quiet you with His love; He will rejoice over you with singing. (Zephaniah 3:17, NIV)

That does not say that God rejoices when we do things well, when we sing just the right notes. He rejoices over us, period. We are His.

This point was brought home to me a few years ago at, of all things, a funeral. Grant Cunningham was my age. We met the first day of Welcome Week at Baylor University. You could not miss his absurdly curly red hair or his infectious grin. Seven years later, we found ourselves, both married by now, as members of the same church in Nashville. I had gone to Nashville to practice law. Grant had gone there, like so many others, to write music.

Unlike so many others, Grant was good at it. He was very good. (In Nashville, we called him "real good.") He won Dove Awards. Earlier in this book, I have quoted the wonderful lyrics from a song called "The Great Divide." Grant wrote that one.

And then, at the age of thirty-seven, with twin two year old boys waiting for him at home, Grant died in a freak accident.

I will never, ever forget Grant's funeral. The music scene in Nashville can produce much in the way of cynicism and me-first oneupsmanship, but there was none of that to be seen that day. The outpouring of love and respect could not be contained. The biggest names in contemporary Christian music were there. Some, like Michael W. Smith and Nicole Nordeman, sang in the service because Kristin asked them to. Others were there simply to cry and worship in a memorial for their friend.

But then something happened that I had never seen before in a funeral service. After Pastor Scotty Smith finished preaching a powerful, evangelistic message to which Grant would have said "Amen," Scotty moved to the side, the lights dimmed, and a screen descended from the ceiling. The projector came on, and we saw Grant's face. It was a videotape of Grant singing, apparently at a writer's night showcasing some new material, the song that turned out to be his last #1 hit. You may know the song "Blue Skies."

I know it sounds hokey, but you will have to trust me when I tell you that it was heart-rending to see Grant's face and hear his voice sing his words from a screen suspended over his closed casket.

When the song was over and the screen went dark, the room sat in hushed reverence. Then, without a script or a prompting, I saw Grant's father stand up on the front row and begin to clap. Just standing there, his back to the thousand or so people in the room looking at… what? The casket? The blank screen? His own tears? I am not sure… and standing alone and clapping. I was devastated. It was a father's applause for the life's work of his son. We in the room were transfixed, for this was not an ovation for a great singing job. I promise you that Point of Grace sings "Blue Skies" far better than Grant could

188

ever have hoped to sing it. Instead, we were witnessing a father watching his son's last performance and showing his unashamed approval.

Don't miss the message. Our Father is rejoicing over us. When we come to the end and the tape of our life's accomplishments is played, it will not matter how well we sang. What matters is that we are His. He will review the tape and stand and applaud and hand us our crown of glory and honor.

How great is the love the Father has lavished on us, that we should be called children of God! And that is what we are! (1 John 3:1, NIV)

He is everlasting God, and we are His.

The Love Chapter comes as the climax of Paul's description to the Corinthians of the gifts we have been given. On top of the gifts of teaching or healing or preaching or interpretation, we have been given the gift of agape. We approach agape only through the transforming power of the Holy Spirit. The attributes of love are goals toward which our Christian walk is aimed. But even more than that, we have been given the greatest gift of all - God. And God is love. How fortuitous!

The Deeper Magic of Forgiveness

Have mercy on me, O God, according to your unfailing love; according to your great compassion blot out my transgressions. Wash away all my iniquity and cleanse me from my sin. For I know my transgressions, and my sin is always before me. (Psalm 51:1-3, NIV)

Sometimes, we have to hit our knees. More often than we confess, we need to confess. Too often, we are again at the throne of God begging not for judgment, not for fairness, not for what we are due, but for mercy. *Kyrie elaison.* Lord, have mercy.

"Lord, I am a sinner. I have failed you. My heart is not pure and my spirit has abandoned its walk with you. I am no more steadfast than the shifting breeze of summer."

Kyrie elaison. Lord, have mercy.

"Dear God, I am guilty of sins that no one but you knows, and in my darkest times, I fear that you will cast me from your presence. I know that is what I deserve. But I desire, I long for, I thirst for your Holy Spirit now more than ever."

Kyrie elaison. Lord, have mercy.

"Oh Jesus, I have no joy. You have saved me, and I know that, but I live as if I did not know it, just as if I were still lost. I deserve my misery, but I beg for your joy."

Kyrie elaison. Lord, have mercy.

"My sin is ever before me. The misdeeds of my hands and my hurtful, dishonest words pale in comparison to the transgressions of my heart. Oh God. I ache with the pain of my sin. And there is nothing that I can do to cleanse myself."

Kyrie elaison. Lord, have mercy.

"Lord, the world was no help to me, so I have tried all of the church's answers. Rituals, service, songs, events, sacrifice of my time for activities to help others – still, my heart is heavy. My heart is broken.

"Could it be that my heart must break?"

Kyrie elaison. Lord, have mercy.

"God, I am beginning to hear you. Finally, I can glimpse a bit of what you are saying to me. I have to see, and admit, the crimson of my wickedness in order to point it out to you and ask you to cleanse it."

Kyrie elaison. Lord, have mercy.

He made you alive together with Him, having forgiven us all our transgressions, having canceled out the certificate of debt consisting of decrees against us and which was hostile to us; and He has taken it out of the way, having nailed it to the cross. (Colossians 2:13-14, NAS)

We know that a holy God's very being cannot abide the presence of sin. So, before we can have a relationship with Him, before we can be called children of God, before we can escape the slavery of evil darkness, we must be freed from the bonds of sin, for we cannot save ourselves. Something has to happen to make us like God – perfect, holy, good. The cry of *"Kyrie elaison"* is the plea for that something. That something is forgiveness.

I have already mentioned C.S. Lewis's classic *The Lion, the Witch, and the Wardrobe*. It is worth mentioning again. If you have not read it, I suggest you put this book down and go read it right now. It will not take you long.

In the story, Edmund leaves his relationship with his brother and sisters and with Aslan, the great lion, when he is seduced by the lifestyle offered him by the White Witch. In order for Edmund to overcome his folly and return to a state of grace with his family, King Aslan allows himself to be captured by the White Witch in exchange for the release of Edmund. This happens in the chapter entitled "Deep Magic from the Dawn of Time." Edmund is once again a brother of Peter, Susan, and Lucy despite his earlier choice, although the deal costs Aslan his life at the hands of the White Witch. The shedding of Aslan's blood on the Stone Table is necessary for Edmund's wanderings to be forgiven and for the White Witch's hold on him to be released.

Fortunately, the book is not over. There is another chapter: "Deeper Magic from Before the Dawn of Time." Aslan is stronger than death. He breaks the bonds that hold him, and the White Witch is defeated. Get the incredible sense of that. When you feel the clutches of this world and your own failures grab you, remember the God who asked Job, "Where were you when I was creating the world?" Remember that God made the rules and runs the show, and just because you have failed does not mean that the game is over. Failure may have cost everything in the way the world has run from the beginning, but the Ruler is not bound by the beginning. I AM always has been, and He is the source of the Deeper Magic.

The ironies that surround the cross (the Stone Table for Aslan) must be examined when we find ourselves pondering the Deeper Magic. As Aslan allows the Witch to take him, this One who created the world and made the rules actually chose to die.

- The holy, sinless man introduced Himself to sin.
- The loving, gentle Jesus endured scorn, hatred, curses, jeers.
- The personification of joy and bringer of hope became acquainted with grief and agony.
- The Creator allowed His own destruction.
- The worker of miracles, the giver of life, chose a path of death.
- The landlord of heaven descended to the gates of hell.
- The commander of demons and resister of the tempter voluntarily paid the ransom of sin.
- The immortal God, who cannot die, died.

That Barabbas was released while Jesus was crucified is irony. That Jesus died so that all of us might live is stupefying.

How often we forget this story. We lose sight of the fact that we have already won the war, that the Deeper Magic of Christ's redeeming love means that despite our choices and our sins, irrespective of our fears and our giving in to the seductions of this world, God's mighty arm has already saved us. We are forgiven.

Despite our sins, we live in God's light and walk in His love. The very mind of Christ is in us, and the power that conquered death is ours. As forgiven sinners, we can share the gift of mercy with others. Because of forgiveness, we can have relationship with God Himself.

This is our reason to sing. With grateful hearts and with the joy of the redeemed, we sing that God has forgiven us.

"Lord, you do cleanse me. You do have mercy. I am, in spite of myself, whiter than the snow."

Kyrie elaison. Lord, you do have mercy on us.

We praise you, *Kyrie.*

God's Blessing for You... Just for You

The God who created life is the God who creates new life. That is the gospel.

The God who created life is the God who recreates life within us. That is grace.

The God who created life is the God who takes what we give Him and renews us, creating from our humble offerings something that only He can imagine; only He can design. That is consecration.

Do not get lost. On your spiritual knees before the throne in your heart, make the commitments called for by a prayer of consecration and blessing, and unleash in yourself the creative powers of the master of the universe.

Jesus gave us the model prayer, and it can mean so much if we look at its words in the context of what God wants to create in us and how He waits to bless us individually. Will you pray with me now?

"Bless my mind. Lead me not into temptation, but keep me focused on you. Help me see with the eyes of the Galilean the hurt that is around me. Give me the wisdom to feel what you feel and understand what you plan for my allotted minutes.

"Sanctify my heart. Deliver me from evil. Shine your endless love through me so that my corner of earth may begin to appear like heaven above.

"Anoint my will, and let Thy will be done. As the only one to create and know the perfect way, enter my secret places and guard me from myself.

"Now, take me, for that is all I have to give. And give I must, if I am to approach surrender to Your plan. For Thine is the kingdom and the power and the glory."

God has chosen to do some of His best work through us. He does not snap His celestial fingers to make buildings appear or to call the hearts of His children to Himself. Instead, He calls us to give back what He has created in us. The Stradivarius violin requires Antonio, the Schwoebel anthem requires David, and the Czechoslovakian altar call requires Billy Graham.

Amazingly, this book requires me. Not that I am Billy Graham or Ernest Hemingway; to the contrary, I am an ordinary man, but I happen to be the ordinary man to whom God has given these words and through whom He expects them to come to you.

There is something that requires you, just as your are. The Creator of the universe is waiting to enter, to renew, and to create. We are His, and we have heard His voice. If we will humble ourselves, and pray, and seek His face, He will answer and forgive and create.

"I hear and follow your sovereign call. Hallowed be Thy name."

The Value of God

I do not practice bankruptcy law or banking law, but that does not keep me off the mailing lists of some of my city's businesses that want lawyers to hire them to "value" companies, property, and other assets. I often receive expensively-printed booklets about "asset valuation" and the process of determining what something is worth so that a company can be sold for the proper amount or so a court can dispose of something appropriately. I do not need these services often for my type of law practice, but getting these mass mailings does tend to make me think about "value" and "worth."

> *You are worthy, our Lord and God, to receive glory and honor and power, for you created all things, and by your will they were created and have their being.* (Revelation 4:11, NIV)

What is God worth?

It is a ridiculous question, of course. He is, after all, the only friend a sinner has. He has been our help in times past and is our hope for years to come. He is the source of every blessing. He gives us peace.

So what is that worth to you?

Ken Holland has written a song in which a man says, "I'd like to buy three dollars worth of God, please." Not enough to fill my soul or to make me love my brother, but just enough to make me look good and feel pleased with myself.

Jesus did not mess around with partial commitments or insignificant gifts to God. He talked about concepts like taking up our cross and losing our lives in order to gain our souls. He has standing to make such statements. After all, He gave His life and took the sins of the world with Him.

So what is God worth to you? Reverence? Fear? Honor? Praise? Are you willing to bow you head and bend your knee to anything? Do you find it easy within you to proclaim Him master and lord?

The ongoing creative process of the Father is amazing. Not only is He Creator, the one who made the world and all of us in it from nothing, but He is Savior, source of our life without end through our knowledge of His son. Even still, He is Sustainer, giving us our next breath and producing growth and experience in each of us.

What is that worth to you?

To worship is to accept and embrace a position of lowly insignificance in comparison to the one worshiped and to offer all that you are in praise, adoration, and awe to that one. I think it is rare that many people truly worship. I treasure true worship, whether I find it in my own church or see it in the face of one I have never met.

"Lift up your heads, O gates, and lift them up, O ancient doors, that the King of glory may come in!" (Psalm 24:9 NAS)

At the end of "A Few Good Men," there is a single moment of recognition, as Tom Cruise's character, a navy lawyer, leaves his newly respectful clients. One client, Corporal Harold Dawson, stands and commands his subordinate "Ten-hut. There's an officer on deck."

There is a similar moment in the classic novel To Kill a Mockingbird and the movie of the same name. The trial is over, and Atticus Finch is making his way out of the courtroom. His daughter is in the balcony watching the trial with the African American townspeople. All of a sudden, she notices that they are all on their feet. Reverend Sykes says to her, in what has been called the greatest line of American literature, "Miss Jean Louise, stand up. Your father's passin'."

As we contemplate worship and the value of God, think back to another single moment. These people were Jews, whose homeland was occupied by a ruling, God-ignoring, Roman army. Their past was, in the long term, covenant and golden calf, exodus and exile; in the near term, it was Pharisees, Passover, drought, and ritualistic waiting for a legendary Messiah. And their future? Within mere days it would be a mob, a so-called trial, and demands for a crucifixion.

But now, Jesus is riding by. It is the most unlikely of circumstances. He rode into the teeth of the enemy soldiers, into the haven of the scheming Sanhedrin, on the back of a borrowed donkey, with a ragtag bunch of followers, only a handful of whom will dare to stand at the foot of the cross five days hence. But at this moment, Jesus is riding by. The people called out "Hosanna."

It can be a single moment for you today. Your life may be full of misery, illness, distrust, and hardship. You certainly do not know what is coming tomorrow. Your past is characterized by rejection, sin, failure, abuse (whether you were the abuser or the victim), and loss. Your future may, even within days, include your being caught up in things you cannot now imagine, and you may find yourself on the wrong side of the wrong fight. You may want to hide now for fear of what you will do later this week.

But at this moment, irrespective of your past and your future, notwithstanding your present circumstances, you find yourself face to face with the living God. In the most unlikely of circumstances, while you are reveling in your sin or hiding in your shame or floundering in your loss, Jesus has arrived. While you decide in this moment how to value His presence, He is in front of you. Jesus is riding by. Corporal Dawson would snap "Ten-hut."

It is the single moments that define eternity – Abraham's hand raised above the boy Isaac, Peter's step onto mere water, Gideon's stop beside a stream, Andrew's peek inside one boy's lunchbox, the centurion's second glance at an execution.

For a group of children and palm branch wavers, and for us, that moment is now. We do not worship because of what we are. We certainly do not celebrate what we have done and been. Our futures are probably not worth a single Hosanna. But, Jesus is riding by.

We do not worship because God has given us many things or because He, our Redeemer, has done great things. He has done them and He will continue to do them, but we would worship Him even if He did not.

We worship because He is worth it. Wonderful counselor, comforter, friend. Almighty king of all kings. Worthy.

Perhaps an image of a soldier or a preacher from a movie can become your watchword every time you come to worship. For indeed, you are entering the very presence of the living God. What will you do with that moment? Do not let Jesus ride by without a Hosanna. For surely this is the Son of God.

Lift up your head. Stand up. Ten-hut. Jesus is riding by.

Now unto the King Eternal, Immortal, Invisible

Now unto the King eternal, immortal, invisible, the only wise God, be honour and glory for ever and ever. Amen. (1 Timothy 1:17, KJV)

Legalese - don't you hate it? You are asked to sign a form and find fine print on the back of the paper in language that you do not understand.

Trust me, I agree with you. I am trained in how to read the stuff, and I hate it. I even write it sometimes, and I hate it. Why do lawyers say, "The party of the first part has a probable intention of entering into a contractual relationship with the party of the second part, the party of the first part's prospective employer, which relationship, if in fact consummated, would commence on the Monday next following the first Sunday of the month for an agreed upon compensation amount and other consideration as set forth therein" when they could say that "Joe wants to go to work for the company next week"?

But I suppose legalese has its place. It has arisen out of old language that is no longer popular, but some legalese – like "proximate cause" and "assumption of the risk" and "res ipsa loquitur" – has very important meaning in today's world.

Many of the words of Paul, especially when we read them in the King James translation, are not as popular today as they once were. His benedictional description of God – the King eternal, immortal, invisible, the only wise God – is foreign to many today, even to many Christians. It is fashionable in our current sensitivities to focus on "Dear God," our best friend, the "Man upstairs." We tend to a familiar, even intimate relationship with God. After all, it was Christ Himself who taught us to pray as to our own father.

In the midst of our private and close relationship with the Father, there is the danger of allowing our salvation experience to become commonplace, ordinary, and even mundane. We miss the miracle of spring and the wonder of the cocoon, and we lose all touch with that great King James phrase: "the fear of the Lord."

When my Dad prays publicly, he always begins by addressing "Almighty God," and he always uses the "thou"s and "thy"s of the King James Version of scripture. We who are listening are reminded of the God whose true mighty nature we cannot begin to comprehend.

Not only is our God our comforter and our friend, He is the immortal author and finisher of our faith. He is our almighty king who wastes nothing, rules over His creation, and gives life to each of us.

Because He is invisible to us, it is easy for us to create Him in our image as we chat with Him (instead of really praying) and as we go to church (instead of entering into the presence of the Father of glory). He is invisible not because He is small or without substance or absent; He is invisible to us because our puny eyes cannot see Him. His splendor makes Him inaccessible to our merely human sight.

Worship involves more than a warm fuzzy emotional experience for us. Worship is the praise of the name of the one who is so far beyond what we can even imagine that He is immortal and invisible.

Give the seventeenth century exalted language a chance. Think about the immortal, invisible, eternal, only wise God. Meditate on Him. If you will, I give you permission never again to have to read "the party of the first part!"

Meekness and Majesty

One final thought about practicing law – I want to win. That is why I am a trial lawyer, a litigator, a "defender" of my clients and their interests. I love to win. I want the jury to come back into the courtroom and tell the world that I am right and my client should get what she wants and that the other side loses.

I take the concept of "zealous representation" of my clients very seriously, and I pull out all the stops. There is nothing wrong with that. It is my job.

But we can take it too far. The people of Israel wanted a winner, a victorious king, so badly that many of them missed Jesus as He walked among them, occasionally on top of the water, healing their sick and raising their dead. The Pharisees waited for a champion to overcome all oppression of the Jews, and while they waited, they passed the time by ordering the crucifixion of a man who was concerned not with their kingdom, but with an eternal, unshakable kingdom.

We read this:

And behold, with the clouds of heaven One like a Son of Man was coming, and He came up to the Ancient of Days and was presented before Him. And to Him was given dominion, Glory and a kingdom, that all the peoples, nations, and men of every language might serve Him. His dominion is an everlasting dominion which will not pass away; and His kingdom is one which will not be destroyed. (Daniel 7:13-14, NAS)

And then there is this:

Blessed are the meek: for they shall inherit the earth. (Matthew 5:5, KJV)

This. . .

But you will receive power when the Holy Spirit comes on you... (Acts 1:8, NIV)

But then this. . .

But the fruit of the Spirit is ... gentleness. (Galatians 5:22-23, NAS)

It is in these words penned by Terry York that I find the enigma of our savior best spoken: "What meekness and what majesty - the cross, the stall, yet deity. I bow to you who bowed to be my Savior and my Lord."

The story of Christ, and of salvation, creation, and the love of the omnipotent master of the universe for us sinful creatures is a paradox, a riddle, a contradiction in terms. He is a king of an unshakable dominion, who is worthy of worship, yet one who leads His flock like a shepherd. We look for the majesty of the conqueror, the Creator, the judge; and indeed He possesses such majesty. In the end, though, it was not His majesty that saved our souls. Nor was it weakness, or defeat, or loss. It was meekness, patient submission, voluntary giving of what could not be taken from Him.

It is the divine paradox that the only perfect one died the death reserved for the worst sins, yours and mine. It is the ridiculous, and miraculous, plan of God that our Lord – He who rules over us and has discretion over even our next breath – became our Savior – He who gave what had to be given to rescue us from ourselves.

It is flabbergasting for us who expect immediate crowns and mansions, for those of us who love to win and want to be seen as winners, that we are to be meek. Like the ancients, we have wanted to ride to victory on warriors' steeds as we leave our mockers in our wake. Instead, we hear Jesus call us to be like He is - voluntarily, patiently submissive.

Meekness is not frail, feeble, flabby, defectiveness of strength, will, or endurance. To be sure, none of us thinks of our Savior as feeble and defective. Nor is gentleness a euphemism for inexperienced, weak, passive inaction.

Gentleness is bowing from your deserved place in order to save those who do not deserve saving. Meekness is the Deity, in all His majesty, deigning to enter an unholy sinful world in a cattle stall, with a cross to look forward to.

Let us remember not only His majesty, but let us tell of the beautiful mystery of His death for us.

For in His death are we all winners. About that, we can all be zealous!

About the Author

Lyn Robbins is senior general attorney for a major national corporation, responsible for overseeing lawsuits and litigation strategy. He works in the creation and development of litigation strategy and in formulating policy to prevent future claims and lawsuits. In addition, he is an adjunct professor of law at Baylor University School of Law and a faculty member of the National Association of Railroad Trial Counsel's College of Trial Advocacy. Previously, he practiced law with a major Nashville, Tennessee law firm, and before that, he was an assistant university debate coach. Mr. Robbins earned his J.D., cum laude, in 1990 from Baylor School of Law, where he was a Leon Jaworski Scholar. He earned his B.A., with honor, in 1987 from Baylor University, where he was a member of the national championship debate team and the first individual debater ever to win the nation's Top Speaker award for two consecutive years. He is certified as a Civil Trial Specialist by the National Board of Trial Advocacy and is listed in Who's Who in America *and* Who's Who in American Law. *He is admitted to practice before a number of courts, including the United States Supreme Court.*

Lyn has been involved in several churches as deacon, Sunday School teacher, retreat leader, choir member, handbell choir director and soloist, church attorney, and committee member. He has spoken to congregations in several states.

Lyn has a number of religious and legal publications. He is also published as a lyricist.

He is a baseball fan who enjoys acting in and directing plays and musicals, going to movies, and reading. He was once a semi-successful contestant on "Who Wants to be a Millionaire?"

CPSIA information can be obtained at www.ICGtesting.com

261187BV00006B/1/P